I0799531

SECRETS OF A FRUITFUL HEART

Tools for Spiritual Growth
from Jesus' Parable of the Sower

BOB SORGE

Oasis House
Kansas City, Missouri

SECRETS OF A FRUITFUL HEART: Tools for Spiritual Growth from Jesus' Parable of the Sower

Published by Oasis House
PO Box 522
Grandview, MO 64030-0522
816-767-8880

ISBN: 978-1-937725-69-3

Editor: Edie Mourey
Cover design: Jessica Beedle
Typesetter: Dale Jimmo

Stay connected with Bob at:
fruitfulheart.net
oasishouse.com
YouTube.com/bobsorge
Facebook.com/BobSorgeMinistry
Blog: bobsorge.com
Instagram: bob.sorge
Twitter.com/BOBSORGE

Contents

PART FIVE: THIRTY—SIXTY—HUNDRED

PART ONE

THE PARABLE INTRODUCED

Parable of the Sower

Then He taught them many things by parables, and said to them in His teaching: "Listen! Behold, a sower went out to sow. And it happened, as he sowed, that some seed fell by the wayside; and the birds of the air came and devoured it. Some fell on stony ground, where it did not have much earth; and immediately it sprang up because it had no depth of earth. But when the sun was up it was scorched, and because it had no root it withered away. And some seed fell among thorns; and the thorns grew up and choked it, and it yielded no crop. But other seed fell on good ground and yielded a crop that sprang up, increased and produced: some thirtyfold, some sixty, and some a hundred." And He said to them, "He who has ears to hear, let him hear!" But when He was alone, those around Him with the twelve asked Him about the parable. And He said to them, "To you it has been given to know the mystery of the kingdom of God; but to those who are outside, all things come in parables, so that 'Seeing they may see and not perceive, and hearing they may hear and not understand; lest they should turn, and their sins be forgiven them.' And He said to them, "Do you not understand this parable? How then will you understand all the parables? The sower sows the word. And these are the ones by the wayside where the word is sown. When they hear, Satan comes immediately and takes away the word that was sown in their hearts. These likewise are the ones sown on stony ground who, when they hear the word, immediately receive it with gladness; and they have no root in themselves, and so endure only for a time. Afterward, when tribulation or persecution arises for the word's sake, immediately they stumble. Now these are the ones sown among thorns; they are the ones who hear the word, and the cares of this world, the deceitfulness of riches, and the desires for other things entering in choke the word, and it becomes unfruitful. But these are the ones sown on good ground, those who hear the word, accept it, and bear fruit: some thirtyfold, some sixty, and some a hundred" (Mark 4:2-20).

CHAPTER 1

Greatest Parable of All Time

Get ready to explore the most brilliant and helpful parable in the entire Bible!

Jesus dubbed it the *parable of the sower* (Matt 13:18), and it serves as His model for discipleship. Everything you need to know about being a disciple of Jesus has been embedded in one profound parable!

That statement is no exaggeration. It's the ultimate Bible passage for making discipleship understandable and doable. It's a one-stop guide that contains every secret for being a fruitful follower of Jesus.

It plays like a movie. It gives us vivid imagery for how our hearts grow as disciples of Christ. When we grow Jesus' way, our hearts become as fruitful to God as a banner wheat harvest.

Jesus' Sledgehammer Parable

The parable of the sower is Jesus' sledgehammer parable. Like Solomon's superlative Song of Songs, this is the Parable of Parables. It's the big one, the most significant, the most magnificent, the GOAT (Greatest Of All Time). It's Jesus' tour de force, His blockbuster, His kingpin. This Mount Everest of parables beckons us to explore its heights.

When you grasp what Jesus infused into this parable and put it into practice, you'll find yourself on heaven's superhighway of discipleship.

Prepare to ponder kingdom secrets you've never seen before. It's about to get real good. We're going to sit at Jesus' feet and thrill at the wisdom of His words.

If you read this book in sincerity and truth, I promise you'll never say to yourself, *This parable doesn't apply to my life right now.* Why? Because it's universally relevant. It doesn't matter your age, gender, marital status, ethnicity, income bracket, placement on the org chart, or how long you've been a Jesus follower, this parable is going to nail you. It doesn't matter what season you're in—whether happy or hard. Makes no difference, this parable is for you. You've been waiting for this.

Master of Metaphor

Get ready for plenty of metaphors. A *metaphor is a word picture that uses an object to explain an idea.* Jesus is the Master of Metaphor. Whether at a meal, a meeting, or a meadow, the greatest Teacher of all time used metaphor in all His messaging, and the metaphors within our parable are the strongest of His entire ministry.

John the Baptist, Jesus' forerunner, used metaphors prolifically to prepare people for Jesus' teaching style. For example, look at the metaphors in this excerpt from John the Baptist:

> **But when he saw many of the Pharisees and Sadducees coming to his baptism, he said to them, "Brood of vipers! Who warned you to flee from the wrath to come? Therefore bear fruits worthy of repentance, and do not think to say to yourselves, 'We have Abraham as our father.' For I say to you that God is able to raise up children to Abraham from these stones. And even now the ax is laid to the root of the trees. Therefore every tree which does not bear good fruit is cut down and thrown into the fire. I indeed baptize you with water unto repentance, but He who is coming after me is mightier than I, whose sandals I am not worthy to carry. He will baptize you with the Holy Spirit and fire. His winnowing fan is in His hand, and He will thoroughly**

> **clean out His threshing floor, and gather His wheat into the barn; but He will burn up the chaff with unquenchable fire" (Matt 3:7-12).**

Vipers, fruits, stones, ax, root, trees, fire, winnowing fan, threshing floor, wheat, barn, chaff. They're all metaphors. That's a mighty muckle of metaphors mashed into one message!

When Jesus talked metaphors, the people probably thought, *This reminds us of John the Baptist.* This is how he talked. They knew to pay attention.

Like John, Jesus' use of metaphors was brilliant, and they shine the brightest in the parable of the sower.

The Parable in a Chart

The following chart encapsulates the message of the parable. It helps us *see* the parable. Refer to it frequently as you ponder the parable's significance. To keep it before you, we'll reproduce it repeatedly throughout this book.

When you actually see the parable, you'll see everything in life through the lens of fruitfulness. You'll constantly be asking, *Is this pursuit fruitful?*

We Want to Be More Fruitful

Fruitfulness was a common theme in Jesus' teachings. He likened our hearts to a spiritual garden that produces fruit pleasing to God. For disciples, fruitfulness is as important as it was to Jesus.

Nobody reading this book is thinking, *No, I don't want to move forward. I want to remain stagnant, myopic, and self-centered.*

Rather, we all want more impact, a deeper imprint, an enduring legacy. We want our lives to make an eternal difference in others. We aspire to be more productive, more

Chart 1
Four Kinds of Soil

FOUR SOILS	HINDRANCE	MAIN ISSUE	CROP	TOOL
Trampled Heart	Birds	Unbelief	Stolen	Hoe
Shallow Heart	Stones	Tolerated Sin	Scorched	Shovel
Neglected Heart	Weeds	Distractions	Choked	Sickle
Fruitful Heart	All three	30/60/100-Fold	Productive	All three

helpful, and giving more glory to our heavenly Father.

But even though we want to be fruitful, we're weak and need encouragement to keep reaching for more. That's why this parable is so helpful. Jesus is going to incentivize us, through the power of His word and the release of His grace, to keep reaching for greater fruit.

Study this parable with a good heart and Jesus will use the vision of hundredfold fruitfulness to fill you with many holy desires:

- You'll want to be more like Jesus, bearing fruit to God everywhere you go (John 15:8).
- You'll strive for hundredfold fruitfulness, producing eternal life in others (John 4:36).
- You'll seek to glorify God more by bearing much fruit (John 15:8).
- You'll want to bear fruit that *remains* because you want to touch answered prayer (John 15:16).
- You'll desire to be more fruitful with age, making your elderly years more productive than ever (Ps 92:14). The older the vine, the sweeter the fruit.
- You'll long to hear Jesus say, "Well done," when He rewards the faithfulness of His servants (Matt 25:21).
- You'll want to gain for the Lamb the reward of His sufferings. His sacrifice deserves ours.

You're using this book to study the parable of the sower because you want to be more fruitful. Tune your ears and lean in attentively. During this study, Jesus will provide practical tools to cultivate a more productive heart in faith and love.

Hundredfold fruitfulness is before you!

CHAPTER 2

The Parable Presented

FOUR SOILS	HINDRANCE	MAIN ISSUE	CROP	TOOL
Trampled Heart	Birds	Unbelief	Stolen	Hoe
Shallow Heart	Stones	Tolerated Sin	Scorched	Shovel
Neglected Heart	Weeds	Distractions	Choked	Sickle
Fruitful Heart	All three	30/60/100-Fold	Productive	All three

Let's look at the parable as presented by Jesus in Mark 4:2-8.

> **Then He taught them many things by parables, and said to them in His teaching: "Listen! Behold, a sower went out to sow" (Mark 4:2-3).**

Jesus launched the parable with a double imperative: **"Listen! Behold."** This marked the strongest language of His entire ministry to underscore a particular teaching. It was as though He grabbed a marker and highlighted the parable in boldface. The urgency of His command demands our attention.

The first word out of His mouth was, *Listen!* It's an injunction—a thunderous charge. He was commanding us to wake up and think. We must gather our minds, block every distraction, and unclog our ears. Whatever you do, hear this one.

The second charge to His audience was, *Behold.* He was about to paint a picture, and He wanted them to open their eyes and see it. If they could visualize the parable with the eyes of their understanding, then its message would be burned indelibly upon their hearts.

Powerful things happen when you *hear and see* Jesus' words. One of my goals in this book, therefore, is to help you both hear and see this parable. When you do, you'll be changed by the power of its message.

At this very moment, Jesus is giving you the same charge He gave His disciples. You're stepping into the greatest of all parables, and He's commanding you with regal authority, *Listen! Behold.*

I've called this Jesus' sledgehammer parable because no other is as life-transformational. It will sift misplaced priorities and establish unshakable foundations for fruitfulness (Heb 12:27). Therefore, open your eyes and ears. If you both *hear* and *see* this parable, it will mark your heart and transform you eternally.

What do the metaphors in the parable represent?

The sower in the parable represents Jesus—or anyone spreading the word in partnership with Him. The seed is the word of God. The soil represents the hearts of hearers. Jesus described four types of soil, and they represent four ways that people hear and respond to the word of God.

Trampled Soil

The first type of soil Jesus introduced was trampled soil.

> **And it happened, as he sowed, that some seed fell by the wayside; and the birds of the air came and devoured it (Mark 4:4).**

The wayside was a footpath running alongside a farmer's field. In Jesus' day, farmers provided a pathway for foot traffic through their fields because they didn't want them rambling randomly or crisscrossing willy-nilly through their fields and damaging their crops. But travelers were permitted to walk across a farmer's property if they kept carefully to the footpath. Called *the wayside* by Jesus, this footpath was a dirt road that facilitated the movement of foot traffic.

Travelers with livestock in tow did their best to keep their cattle on the narrow confines of the wayside lest, wandering off the path, the animals should trample the farmer's crops.

In verse four, Jesus pictured a farmer scattering seed with the toss of his hands. Some of the seed fell on the footpath, but when it hit the hardened surface, the seed just bounced and sat on top of the ground. When the birds saw the seed on the surface, they swooped and enjoyed an easy meal.

Later, Jesus explained that the birds symbolize demons stealing the word of God from hard hearts (Mark 4:15).

The wayside soil represents what I'm calling *the Trampled Heart*, someone who hears but doesn't understand due to a hardened heart.

Shallow Soil

Then Jesus introduced the second kind of soil—shallow soil.

> **Some fell on stony ground, where it did not have much earth; and immediately it sprang up because it had no depth of earth. But when the sun was up it was scorched, and because it had no root it withered away (Mark 4:5-6).**

Like a barricade, stones hinder seeds from lodging deeply enough in the soil and impede roots from descending. If a seed is shallow in the soil, it will sprout shoots more quickly because they don't have to push through a heavy layer of soil. This gives the appearance of robust, eager growth. But that appearance of healthy growth is deceptive because stones are blocking the roots from accessing the moisture below. When roots are shallow in the dirt, the sizzling sun will scorch and wither the plant. We're calling this *shallow soil*, but what we really mean is that the seed and roots are shallow. Stones stop seeds and roots from penetrating deeply enough into the moist soil below.

The stony ground represents someone whose response to God's word is shallow, so I'm calling this *the Shallow Heart*.

Neglected Soil

Thirdly, Jesus portrayed neglected soil.

> **And some seed fell among thorns; and the thorns grew up and choked it, and it yielded no crop (Mark 4:7).**

This soil was in a part of the field that was overgrown with thorns and weeds. If a farmer neglects to suppress or control weeds, weeds can overtake a field and choke the harvest.

With *choke*, Jesus used the perfect word. Weeds choke. They choke good plants by depriving them of sunlight, moisture, access to nutrients, and room to grow. Left unchecked, weeds can stifle and destroy a good crop.

The bad stuff always tries to choke the good stuff.

This third category of soil represents what I'm calling *the Neglected Heart* because the farmer had neglected the task of weed management.

Fruitful Soil

Fourthly, Jesus depicted fruitful soil.

> **But other seed fell on good ground and yielded a crop that sprang up, increased and produced: some thirtyfold, some sixty, and some a hundred (Mark 4:8).**

Jesus described this soil as *good* because it yielded a crop. Good soil produces fruit.

With His designations of thirty, sixty, and hundred, Jesus

pointed to three levels of fruitfulness. Most fields have this diversity of productivity. For example, drive past a cornfield and you'll likely see the diversity of thirty, sixty, and hundredfold right from your car. You'll see some cornstalks that are short and stunted, other stalks that are medium in height, and yet others that are tall and strongly developed. The height of the stalk often reflects the health of the plant and portends its fruitfulness.

A novice might suppose that all the corn plants in a given field would be equally fruitful. After all, the plants come from the same variety of seed, they're all planted at the same time, and receive the same rainfall. But even so, some plants are more fruitful than others.

In the same way, disciples of Jesus differ in fruitfulness. Most disciples have access to the same gospel nutrients, and the same Holy Spirit waters, but not all access those resources equally. Even so, Jesus commended all levels of fruitfulness, whether thirtyfold, sixty, or hundred.

This fourth kind of soil represents what I'm calling *the Fruitful Heart.*

Next, Jesus explained why He taught the people in parables.

CHAPTER 3

The Purpose of Parables

After teaching this parable, Jesus met privately that evening with His disciples. As they discussed the events of the day, the disciples were still in the grip of the sower parable. They sensed its message was unusually strong but struggled to grasp its full meaning. Seeking clarity, they asked Jesus to debrief with them:

> **But when He was alone, those around Him with the twelve asked Him about the parable. And He said to them, "To you it has been given to know the mystery of the kingdom of God; but to those who are outside, all things come in parables, so that 'Seeing they may see and not perceive, and hearing they may hear and not understand; lest they should turn, and their sins be forgiven them'" (Mark 4:10-12).**

In response to the disciples' inquiry about the parable, Jesus began by discussing His use of parables in general. He said, "To you it has been given to know the mystery of the kingdom of God." He used the term *mystery* to describe a truth about the kingdom that had been veiled in past generations but was now being unveiled to His chosen disciples.

In His explanation, Jesus introduced a paradox. He said the purpose of parables was to *conceal* and to *reveal.* How can a parable both conceal and reveal at the same time? It's paradoxical.

By the way, whenever you encounter a paradox in the kingdom, pay special attention because some of the most profound truths of the kingdom are found at the vortex of paradox. Look at this paradox with me.

When an *insincere* listener hears a parable, the purpose of the parable is to conceal God's truth from their understanding. But when a *sincere* listener hears it, the parable opens them to the power of Jesus' message. Thus, parables have diametric responses, depending on the hearts of the hearers.

When an insincere listener hears a parable, they're likely to respond with something like, "Now *that's* confusing! That parable is totally abstract. A bunch of mumbo-jumbo, if you ask me. There's no point to the parable."

But when a sincere listener hears a parable, they're likely to say things like, "Wow, that parable makes so much sense! Now I get it. It answers so many questions for me. I can totally see myself in the parable! That's really helpful."

Isaiah's Paradoxical Quote

Isaiah's statement that Jesus quoted is intriguing: "Seeing they may see and not perceive, and hearing they may hear and not understand; lest they should turn, and their sins be forgiven them" (see Isa 6:9-10). Why would God not want someone to turn and their sins be forgiven?

This seems paradoxical to us because we know God is "not willing that any should perish but that all should come to repentance" (2 Pet 3:9). Don't those statements contradict? But here's the thing. God doesn't want people in His kingdom who have checked off the correct boxes but haven't had a genuine change of heart. In other words, Jesus doesn't want people in His kingdom who have entered on a technicality but don't actually love Him.

It's all about love. Jesus wants authentic repentance that produces overflowing love and gratitude for His mercy. Parables have a way of separating those who love from those who don't.

Master Key

Then Jesus continued the conversation.

> **And He said to them, "Do you not understand this parable? How then will you understand all the parables?" (Mark 4:13).**

Jesus spoke of this parable like no other.

He was asking, "If you can't understand this parable, how can you understand any of them?" That question implied that this parable was like a Master Key to unlock understanding in all the parables. Get this one right and doors open to the others.

Clearly, this parable was pivotal!

What makes this parable key to understanding all others? What a fantastic question! While I have only scratched the surface of the answer, one aspect stands out.

Each metaphor in the parable—seed, soil, stones, weeds—contains almost inexhaustible depths of meaning. As you probe each metaphor, your understanding of truth keeps enlarging and you're inspired to keep exploring the metaphors for more.

In other words, this parable shows that we can't put too much pressure on the metaphors. The metaphors don't break under scrutiny, but can sustain the rigors of exacting examination. The harder you squeeze them, the sweeter their fruit. They're inviting us to a *lifetime* of contemplation.

I hear Jesus saying, "You can do this with *all* the parables. You can extract endless possibilities of meaning from the metaphors in all My parables." When we learn to glean meaning from the metaphors in *this* parable, therefore, we're equipped to wring meaning from *all* the parables.

Some argue against extracting more from a parable than its most obvious meaning, but I hear Jesus encouraging us to dig deep. After all, He's had an eternity to craft them meticulously for us.

In Mark 4:13, Jesus was hinting, "There's more to be gleaned from this parable than you could exhaust in a lifetime of study. Go after it. See what you can uncover. The more you mine, the more you'll be enriched."

Next, Jesus explained the parable to His disciples.

CHAPTER 4

The Parable Explained

After clarifying why He used parables, Jesus went on to explain His meaning in this parable. The soil represented the hearts of hearers (Mark 4:15). The four types of soil reflected distinct heart conditions, leading to different responses to the word. First, He explained the response of the hardened wayside soil to the seed—which we're calling *the Trampled Heart*. Here's Jesus' explanation:

> **And these are the ones by the wayside where the word is sown. When they hear, Satan comes immediately and takes away the word that was sown in their hearts (Mark 4:15).**

The Trampled Heart

The wayside was basically a narrow dirt road that bordered a farmer's field. Cultivated crops were probably on both sides, so travelers would stick to the path to avoid damaging the crops. Trodden by many travelers, the surface of the path was trampled hard. In the parable, therefore, the wayside represented a heart that was trampled hard.

When a trampled heart hears the word of God, it's too hardened to believe and receive the word because God's word enters the heart through *faith*. A hard heart, however, can't understand and receive the word by faith. When the word is sown on a hard heart, it just bounces and lays on the surface. Immediately, the birds descend and gobble up the seed.

Jesus indicated that the seed-eating birds represent Satan and his demons. When the word lays on the surface of an unbelieving heart, demons immediately remove those seeds so they don't produce any fruit in the heart. The problem is not with the seed—the seed is good. The problem is that the heart is hardened with unbelief and doesn't receive the word.

Listen. It's a *kindness* when the word of God haunts or troubles you with the strength of its claims. What a blessing—when the word of God puts you in a headlock, wrestles you to the ground, and reduces you to a groaning, agonizing puddle of tears. Why? Because that means the seed gained entrance to your heart and the demons couldn't steal it. Your heart was soft enough for the word to penetrate!

But in the parable, the trampled heart was too hardened to receive the word of faith. The seed that should have fed the heart fed demons.

The Shallow Heart

Next, Jesus went on to explain that the second kind of soil in the parable represented what we're calling *the Shallow Heart.*

> **These likewise are the ones sown on stony ground who, when they hear the word, immediately receive it with gladness; and they have no root in themselves, and so endure only for a time. Afterward, when tribulation or persecution arises for the word's sake, immediately they stumble (Mark 4:16-17).**

In this plot of ground, stones hindered root development by denying the roots access to the damp soil below. Plants need their roots to penetrate deep into the earth so they can absorb the subterranean moisture. If the roots can't reach deep enough, the sun's heat will scorch the plant.

We're calling this soil *the Shallow Heart* because the roots of the plants are shallow in depth. Shallow roots represent a shallow faith, and the sun's heat represents difficulty, trials, persecution, or temptation (see Luke 8:13). When shallow faith is clobbered by adversity or temptation, the roots don't go deep to access the depths of God's love, the heart is scorched, and the person becomes a spiritual casualty.

Notice the word *gladness* in verse 16. This person has an initial response of gladness to God's word. Why? Because their sins are forgiven! They feel the relief of a clean conscience, and they feel the refreshing of God's wonderful promises. It's a happy day! They're weeping, smiling, and laughing—for good reason. They have been washed and cleansed by the power of the gospel!

But their response to the word is mostly emotional. Emotional feelings about God's word are warranted and wonderful but, by themselves, are inadequate for the long haul. A response to the gospel that is only emotional is shallow.

To endure in the faith, the word must go deeper than our emotions. If we're to go the distance, the seed must penetrate deep, reaching into our convictions, values, desires, and will. If God's word merely sparks fleeting emotions, trouble will eventually take us out.

When farmers plow their fields, they frequently encounter stones in the soil. If they're wise, they'll stop, dig up the stones with their shovel, and toss them.

But suppose it's late in the day and the farmer's in a hurry. He hits a stone with his plow but doesn't feel like taking the time to stop and do the hard work of getting that stone out of his field. Or maybe the farmer's tired, and he's just not in the mood to mess with the stone. Imagine the farmer leaving the stone in his field. If he does, that stone will diminish the strength of the harvest.

If a field has enough stones in it, the stones can completely ruin the harvest.

What do the stones represent? *Pockets of sinful compromise.* When we allow a sin in our lives to remain unchallenged, we're leaving a stone in the garden of our hearts. That pocket of sin will hinder our root development and minimize our fruitfulness.

When people make a decision for Christ but then fall away, their ruin is often because of tolerated stones of compromise in their hearts. For example, I've water baptized believers who had great joy in their conversion and gladly entered the waters, but then continued to tolerate pockets of sin in their lives. Consequently, when I went to inquire into their spiritual welfare a little while later, they were not to be found. They were history. Gone. They had no spiritual fruit and were completely disconnected from the family of faith. Why? Because they refused to deal with their stones of sin and compromise. When things got tough, they became spiritual casualties.

In the parable, Jesus was warning us: Stones of tolerated sin can hinder your roots, parch your spiritual vitality, and knock you out.

The Neglected Heart

Next, Jesus explained that the third type of soil in the parable represented what we're calling *the Neglected Heart.*

> **Now these are the ones sown among thorns; they are the ones who hear the word, and the cares of this world, the deceitfulness of riches, and the desires for other things entering in choke the word, and it becomes unfruitful (Mark 4:18-19).**

This soil was overgrown with thorns, the crop was choked, and the ground unfruitful. I'm calling this *the Neglected Heart* because a heart that's overrun with thorns has been neglected. Solomon illustrated that neglect in this proverb:

> **I went by the field of the lazy man, and by the vineyard of the man devoid of understanding; and there it was, all overgrown with thorns; its surface was covered with nettles (Proverbs 24:30-31).**

This proverb described a farmer who was too lazy to suppress the weeds in his vineyard. He had *neglected* his field, and as a result, it was overgrown with nettles. For a field to be fruitful, a farmer must engage aggressively in weed control. But in the proverb, the lazy farmer had neglected that task, and his field was fruitless.

Jesus meant that if a hearer of the word is lazy and neglects to cut back the weeds that threaten to overgrow the heart, their heart is likely to bear little or no fruit.

What do the weeds in the parable represent? Jesus told us plainly. He said the weeds are the natural pursuits of life. When we get distracted with the cares and pleasures of this present world, those pursuits are like weeds that choke the word of God from being fruitful in our hearts.

In this part of the parable, Jesus pitted the temporary against the eternal. All of us feel the tension between the two—between the fruitful and the unfruitful. Something within us wants to devote our lives to the eternal things of the kingdom, but then something else within us wants to enjoy the temporary pleasures of life. The unfruitful distracts us from the fruitful.

When Jesus told us in Matthew 6:33 to seek first the kingdom of God and His righteousness, He was basically saying, "Seek first the fruitful." Why? Because He knew we'd be tempted to focus first on the task of making everyday life work.

The demands and pleasures of everyday life are like weeds that want to overtake our schedules. If we neglect to control those nasty weeds, they'll overgrow the garden of our hearts and diminish our fruitfulness.

The Fruitful Heart

Finally, Jesus explained that the fourth type of soil was good ground, and it represented what we're calling *the Fruitful Heart.*

> **But these are the ones sown on good ground, those who hear the word, accept it, and bear fruit: some thirtyfold, some sixty, and some a hundred (Mark 4:20).**

When the word of God falls on good ground, it penetrates the heart and produces a spiritual harvest.

This verse is talking about *you*! I say that because you're still reading this book. The fact that you've made it this far indicates that you're probably a fruitful Christian. Even if you're only a little bit fruitful, you're still fruitful. You have a good heart, and you're bearing fruit to God.

In the next chapter, I want to identify the linchpin word of the parable.

CHAPTER 5

Four Ways We Hear

Hear is the linchpin word in the parable of the sower. Jesus began the parable with the imperative, "Listen!" (Mark 4:3). And He concluded the parable by urging, "He who has ears to hear, let him hear!" (Mark 4:9). Furthermore, the four heart responses in the parable depended entirely upon how the word was *heard*.

He who has ears to hear, let him hear! That injunction is quintessential Jesus. John used the phrase once in Revelation 13:9, but every other occurrence in Scripture comes exclusively from Jesus. It's almost like the phrase was His trademark.

He who has ears to hear, let him hear! The Gospel writers had Him saying this on seven different occasions (Matt 11:15; 13:43; Mark 4:9; 4:23; 7:16; 8:18; Luke 14:35). Then Jesus spoke it seven times when He addressed the seven churches in Revelation 2-3. That makes for fourteen distinct mentions.

Hearing is the central idea of the entire parable. Let this linchpin word grip you.

FOUR SOILS	HINDRANCE	MAIN ISSUE	CROP	TOOL
Trampled Heart	Birds	Unbelief	Stolen	Hoe
Shallow Heart	Stones	Tolerated Sin	Scorched	Shovel
Neglected Heart	Weeds	Distractions	Choked	Sickle
Fruitful Heart	All three	30/60/100-Fold	Productive	All three

As you look again at Chart 1, the four kinds of soil represent four ways people hear God's word.

First, some hear the word with a hard heart of unbelief. Second, some hear the word with a heart that's so full of compromise (stones) that the plant is scorched. Third, some hear the word with a heart that's so distracted by cares and pleasures (weeds) that eternal fruit is choked. Fourth, some hear the word with a good heart and produce a harvest—some thirtyfold, some sixty, and some a hundred. Whether someone's heart is fruitful or not depends entirely upon how they *hear* the word.

Everything in the parable comes down to hearing.

My Encounter with This Word

I had a powerful encounter with the word *hear*. It was so life-changing that I want to share the story with you.

It happened when I was thirty-seven years old and in a very difficult season personally. My life seemed to be over, and I was desperate to touch Jesus. In my desperation, I decided to do something I had never done before. I went on a twenty-one-day water-only fast. I said to my wife, "I'm going away for twenty-one days to seek the Lord, then I'm coming home to resign as pastor of this church. It's all over." As far as I could see at the time, my profession as a pastor was over, and there was nothing else to go to. My life had seemingly come to an end.

As I embarked on the fast, I said to the Lord, "Who are You, anyway? I don't think I know You, because I never expected You to strip from me every way I've been fruitful in the kingdom. You're taking it all away. Who are You?" I was desperate to know God.

I decided to devote my Scripture reading almost entirely, during those twenty-one days, to the four Gospels. I was desperate to know Jesus, and the only way I knew to get to know Him better was to pore over His words and deeds. I set aside everything I *thought* I knew about Him, and came to the Gospels as though I were a novice reading His story for the first time. My prayer was simply, "Show me who You are."

Some Bibles have the words of Jesus printed in red ink, so if it was red, I was reading it. I immersed myself in Matthew,

Mark, Luke, John, and then Revelation 1-3. Over and over. Hour after hour.

The Trifecta

I didn't realize it at the time, but I had stumbled onto the trifecta of heart transformation. I was doing the three things that, when combined, constitute the secret sauce—the powerful mix for transformational encounter.

Here's the trifecta: Seclusion, word immersion, and fasting. Combine those three things, throw in a good dollop of holy desperation, and you're a holy setup for spiritual revitalization. Let me comment briefly on each of the three elements.

Seclusion. Carve out the time to get away and get alone with Jesus. Do your best to leave behind things that divert, such as professional labors and online activity. The idea is to separate yourself for a season from all that distracts so you can give Jesus your full attention.

Word immersion. Nothing compares to the word of God. It's a hammer, a fire, an irrigator, a refiner, a feeder, a cleanser, a discerner, a light, a plumbline, a lifeline. When we immerse ourselves in the word and the words of Jesus abide in us, that's the alchemy of answered prayer (see John 15:7). There are sixty-six books in the Bible that are worthy of your meditation, but when you get away with Jesus for the first time on a focused prayer retreat such as I'm describing, I recommend immersing yourself first in the words of Jesus.

Fasting. The purpose of fasting is to increase the intensity of our pursuit after Jesus. Fasting helps us respond more deeply to His word and Spirit, which in turn makes us more fruitful.

I was not coached in this trifecta, but the Lord graciously helped me stumble into it. For those with ears to hear, it's completely mind-renewing, heart-softening, and life-transforming.

Most Important Word

While on the retreat and diving deep into the words of Christ, a certain word began to pop off the page at me. I discovered that Jesus used this word frequently in His teaching ministry. Each time He used that word, it impacted my heart. He repeated that word frequently, both in the Gospels and also in Revelation 1-3.

I thought to myself, *Jesus used that word a lot.*

Then it hit me like a freight train: *It's the most important word in the whole Bible*! If, in fact, Jesus emphasized that word most in His teaching ministry, that would make it the most important word in all Scripture.

What was that word? *Hear*. "He who has ears to hear, let him hear." How many times did He say it? Over and over, He emphasized *hearing* in His teachings and parables.

Even the Father confirmed it from heaven when He spoke on the mountain and said, "This is My beloved Son, in whom I am well pleased. *Hear* Him!" (Matt 17:5). How much more emphatic could God possibly be?

And get this: *Hear* is the most important word in the parable of the sower.

In the three Gospel accounts of our parable, the visibility of *hear* in the accounts differs. In Luke's rendering of the parable, *hear* occurs only seven times. In Mark's account, it occurs eight times. In Matthew's record, *hear* occurs a remarkable seventeen times! It's the most important word in the Bible and also in our parable.

Again, understanding that the four soils represent four kinds of heart responses when hearing the word, we realize that the differences in fruitfulness were based entirely upon how the word was heard.

As seen in Chart 1 above, there are four ways people hear God's word:

1. When the trampled heart hears God's word, it's so hardened by unbelief that it's unable to understand and receive the seed of the word. The birds get the seed, and the word is forgotten.

2. When the shallow heart hears God's word, it receives the seed at only an emotional level. When hit by the heat of temptation, trials, and persecution, the plant can't access enough moisture and is scorched.

3. When the neglected heart hears the word, its initial response is receptive, but then it fails to suppress the encroaching weeds. Overcome by the cares and pleasures of life, the plant is choked.

4. When the fruitful heart hears the word, it receives the seed, retains it, puts down roots, sends forth shoots, and bears fruit.

Everything in the parable was based on hearing. It's impossible to overstate the significance of this point. All of us bear fruit to God based on how we hear the word.

Rebuttals

I can imagine someone pushing back and saying, "Well, I don't agree with you, Bob. I think the most important word in the Bible is *love*."

That's great. Love is real important. Never enough love! But there is a passage that says, "Hear, O Israel.…You shall love the LORD your God" (Deut 6:4-5). *Hear* preceded *love*.

Someone else might counter, "Well, I also don't agree with you, Bob. I think the most important word in the Bible is *faith*."

That's great. Faith is real important. I'm always pursuing more faith! There is a verse, however, that says, "Faith comes by hearing" (Rom 10:17). First hearing, then faith.

Hearing comes first. When you hear, now you can repent. When you hear, now you can believe. When you hear, now you can obey. When you hear, now you can change. When you hear, now you can love. When you hear, now you can endure. When you hear, now you can understand. When you hear, now you know whether you should date that guy. When you hear from God, now you know whether you should relocate to that other city.

Everything changes when you hear from God. When you hear from God, keys are released, and doors are opened. One word from God's mouth can be so significant that it can be worth a lifetime of sowing in prayer in order to hear it.

Watch for Every Occurrence

When I perceived that *hear* was the most important word in the Bible, I found myself wanting to underline its occurrence every time I encountered it in Scripture. I'm hoping its significance will hit you the same way. From now on, every time you encounter *hear* in your Bible reading, may it pop off the page and arrest your attention.

Watch for it!

Everything in the Christian walk comes down to hearing and obeying. Decisions come clear when we hear. The greatest treasures in Christ are found through hearing. Hearing is the wellspring of eternal life. It's the fountainhead of kingdom power and authority. It's the source of all wisdom and understanding. It's the basis for hundredfold fruitfulness. Nothing replaces the confidence and authority that comes from hearing God.

The great cry of the awakened believer is, "Let him kiss me with the kisses of his mouth" (Song of Solomon 1:2). What are the kisses of His mouth? They're the words He speaks that feed, strengthen, quicken, and invigorate our hearts. We receive His kisses by hearing His word. When He kisses us with

His word, our hearts spring alive in vibrant fruitfulness.

I love to talk to God, but I love it even more when He talks to me. Things don't change when I talk to God; things change when God talks to me. When I talk, nothing happens; when God talks, universes comes into existence.

We're desperate to hear from God! This is why we spend time daily in the secret place, meditating in His word. Hearing God is our source of life.

Jesus, help me hear Your words with a good heart so that I might bear even more fruit!

But what does it mean to be fruitful? What exactly *is* spiritual fruit? The answer is important because, if we understand clearly what fruit is, then we can pursue it intentionally and become even more fruitful.

Come to the next chapter, therefore, and let's identify spiritual fruit.

CHAPTER 6

What Is Spiritual Fruit?

When we hear and understand this parable, our natural response is, "Lord, I want to be more fruitful!" We have an inherent longing to transcend thirtyfold fruitfulness and reach for more. Every devoted disciple shares this aspiration.

We realize that pursuing greater fruitfulness is a process. There's no such thing as *instant fruit*. By definition, fruit involves gradual growth and is produced through constancy, endurance, and patience. Saying yes to greater fruitfulness means embracing a lifestyle of abiding in Christ and His word. In Luke's version of this parable, Jesus said we "bear fruit with patience" (Luke 8:15).

But what does it mean to be more fruitful? What does spiritual fruit look like? Let me suggest this working definition:

Spiritual fruit is any godly deposit or quality that makes it into the age to come.

Everything in our lives categorizes into either the temporary or the eternal. The temporary fades away when we die; the eternal has value in the age to come. The earthly is fruitless; the heavenly is fruitful.

We are not "men of the world who have their portion in this life" (Ps 17:14). Rather, we've been raised with Christ, are seated with Him in heavenly places, and have set our minds "on things above, not on things on the earth" (Col 3:2).

Defining spiritual fruit based on its endurance aligns with Jesus' statement, "I chose you and appointed you that you should go and bear fruit, and that your fruit should remain" (John 15:16). Spiritual fruit *remains*—that is, it remains *forever*.

The Temporary Can Profit a Little

The conditioning of our physical body is a temporal matter. When we die, whether our body was buff or blubber, none of it is going with us. However, Paul wrote, "Bodily exercise profits a little" (1 Tim 4:8). The body will ultimately perish, but bodily exercise is profitable when it helps us be more fruitful. If we keep our bodies reasonably fit, we'll probably have a little more strength—and maybe even a longer life span—to cultivate spiritual fruit.

Bodily exercise profits a little, but should be practiced with *restraint*. Why? Because we can give it more time than is profitable. A little bit of physical exercise provides a substantial health benefit, making it a little profitable. But much physical exercise doesn't proportionately increase our ability to be fruitful. Rather, it can distract from fruitfulness.

I'll illustrate my meaning with the example of my chainsaw. I love my chainsaw. I love using it so much that I actually have two chainsaws, smile. We have some wooded acreage on our property, and I enjoy harvesting firewood and burning it in our woodstove in winter. When I have my chainsaw in hand, every tree bows, and every limb confesses that I'm lord of my property. When the trees tumble, I pound my chest like a dominating gorilla.

Gathering firewood for winter benefits me in a couple ways. It provides me with the emotional release of a delightful outdoor distraction, and it gives me a good cardiovascular workout. At my age, staying limber and working up a sweat are valuable health benefits. Plus, burning the wood saves on my heating bill.

I love working in the woods so much that, if I were to let myself go, I would be outside with my chainsaw for hours every day—enjoying the outdoors and storing up free firewood. But I realize there are limits to the physical and emotional benefits I gain. Therefore, there comes a time when

I cease. I *restrain* myself. A moment comes when it's time to set the chainsaw aside, get cleaned up, and devote myself instead to that which is truly fruitful.

This parable has changed how I live! It helps me manage my chainsaw, as well as other distractions. The parable has made me aware, more than ever, that the temporary can choke the eternal. It motivates me to devote myself more fully to those things that have an eternal reward.

The Ungodly Bear Bad Fruit

Let me clarify this: The ungodly also bear fruit that will greet them when they die. But in their case, the fruit will be undesirable. Jesus called it *bad fruit*: "Even so, every good tree bears good fruit, but a bad tree bears bad fruit" (Matt 7:17).

Paul wrote about bad fruit when he said that fleshly sins "bear fruit to death" (Rom 7:5; see also 1 Tim 5:24). The point is, *everyone* is fruitful, but not all fruit is good. Some people bear bad fruit that produces death and judgment. We, on the other hand, commit to producing good fruit that remains before God forever.

We're going to look now at some practical examples of spiritual fruit so we can cultivate it more intentionally.

CHAPTER 7

Examples of Fruit

What might be some examples of good fruit? Great question! Let's identify what good kingdom fruit is so we can recognize, value it, and cultivate it.

To explore this, we'll cite ten instances of spiritual fruit in the following two chapters. While this list isn't exhaustive, it serves as a conversation starter. As you grow in Christ, you'll probably identify additional types of spiritual fruit. For now, here are ten examples to consider:

1. Friendship With Jesus

Everything you invest in your friendship with Jesus is eternal. When you die and go to be with Him, your friendship will continue seamlessly. Every aspect of your current friendship will be remembered by Him *forever*. He'll acknowledge the relationship by calling you *friend* (Luke 14:10).

Prayer invests. Prayer invests in a friendship with Jesus. Everything you sow and grow in your friendship with Him—through prayer—is eternal fruit.

Your secret place friendship with Jesus is "the womb of the morning" that produces eternal fruit to God (Ps 110:3).[1]

2. Godly Character

When we're conforming to the image of Christ, we're developing godly character. In Scripture, becoming more like Jesus is called *godliness* (1 Tim 4:7). Godliness is being God-like—that is, demonstrating the virtues of Christ in a growing way. Any Christ-like quality developed in us now is eternal and goes with us into the age to come.

---

1 See my book *Secrets of the Secret Place.*

John the Baptist called on his listeners to develop the fruit of godliness in their lives: "Therefore bear fruits worthy of repentance" (Matt 3:8). If repentance is real, it will bear the fruit of godly character.

When Paul itemized the fruit of the Spirit, it read like a list of Christ's character qualities: "But the fruit of the Spirit is love, joy, peace, longsuffering, kindness, goodness, faithfulness, gentleness, self-control" (Gal 5:22-23). Jesus personifies the fullness of each of these. To the measure we attain these fruit *now* will be the springboard from which we will continue to abound in these character qualities *forever*.

Godly character is true spiritual fruit.

3. Edifying the Body of Christ

Paul said that when the gospel is preached and the body of Christ is strengthened in faith and love, this produces spiritual fruit to God (see Col 1:3-6). Furthermore, he said that when he labored among the churches, it produced fruit from his labor (Phil 1:22; Rom 1:13).

Similarly, when we preach the word and build up the body of Christ, we bear fruit to God. In fact, we're always seeking to become increasingly skillful in edifying the body of Christ. Why? Because the more skillfully we strengthen our brothers and sisters in their faith, the more fruitful we become.

Do you really want to become more fruitful? *Then help other disciples become more fruitful.* When you do, your fruitfulness can be multiplied in others.

4. Winning Souls

Jesus promised to make His disciples "fishers of men" (Matt 4:19). We see one example of that fruitfulness taking place when Peter preached on the day of Pentecost and about three thousand souls were added to their number (Acts 2:41).

Jesus had made Peter a fruitful fisher of men!

Solomon wrote, "The fruit of the righteous is a tree of life, and he who wins souls is wise" (Prov 11:30). The righteous who win souls for Christ are so wise! They're gathering fruit to God.

When someone wanders away, and we turn them back to the truth of Christ, we "save a soul from death and cover a multitude of sins" (James 5:20). Winning a soul in this manner is truly fruitful because we're making a difference in the eternal destiny of a precious soul.

5. Wise Financial Stewardship

One of Christ's most remarkable assertions was that the righteous, through wise financial stewardship, can leverage the rotting resources of this world for eternal fruit (see Luke 16:9; Rom 15:28; Phil 4:17).

Why would I describe this world's resources as *rotting*? Because money is not morally neutral. In Luke 16:9, Jesus called money *unrighteous*, indicating that it has an inherently sinister substance to it. Money never came to us from heaven, but has its derivation in the world's marketplace. When the harlot Babylon is judged, all the world's rotting markets will also be judged (Rev 17:4; 18:3).

What Jesus taught about money was stunning. He said, "Do not lay up for yourselves treasures on earth, where moth and rust destroy and where thieves break in and steal; but lay up for yourselves treasures in heaven, where neither moth nor rust destroys and where thieves do not break in and steal" (Matt 6:19-20). He meant that when we steward our resources wisely—through almsgiving, tithes, and offerings—we can use Babylon's unrighteous riches to store up eternal treasure. The exchange is altogether remarkable!

Kingdom generosity turns mammon into the momentous, the despicable into the delightful, the vile into the valuable, the fruitless into the fruitful.

The righteous are always generous, therefore, because they value eternal fruit—treasure in heaven that will grant them a rich entrance into glory.

This chapter underscores that strengthening our friendship with Jesus, developing Christ-like character, edifying the body of Christ, winning souls, and practicing wise financial stewardship contribute to being fruitful to God.

But there's more. The next chapter will explore even more examples of spiritual fruit.

CHAPTER 8

More Examples of Fruit

In the last chapter, we looked at five examples of spiritual fruit, but there are more. Here are five additional ways to be fruitful in the kingdom of God.

6. Obedience to Jesus

A disciple is someone who is striving to hear and obey everything Jesus commands. Every time you obey Jesus, your obedience is a fruitful fragrance to Him. Wholehearted obedience produces eternal fruit, as John wrote, "He who does the will of God abides forever" (1 John 2:17). Even seemingly small acts, like offering a cup of cold water in obedience, are rewarded (Matt 10:42).

For an act of obedience to be eternally fruitful, it must encompass all aspects of Romans 11:36, "For of Him and through Him and to Him are all things, to whom be glory forever. Amen." Of, through, to. Let's look at all three.

First, for something to be fruitful, it must be *of Him*—that is, it must originate in His heart. We must receive the impetus of the idea from above.

Second, for something to be fruitful, it must be *through Him*—that is, we obey Him through the power He provides (Zech 4:6). Only that which is done through God's enabling grace can be eternally fruitful.

And third, for something to be fruitful, it must be *to Him*—that is, the glory of the exploit must return to God not a human vessel. When our obedience is of Him, done through Him, and returns to Him, then it's fruitful.

7. Providing Security for Your Household

We can bear fruit to God by making our home a spiritual refuge for our children. Their souls are eternal, and when they grow and thrive physically, emotionally, and spiritually, we are bearing fruit to God.

Parents offer security for their households by providing shelter, sustenance, protection, identity, belonging, blessing, and inheritance (Gen 49:26; Prov 1:8; 13:22; Luke 15:31; 1 Thess 2:11). These provisions establish a context of security for children to grow in God, aligning with Paul's assertion that neglecting these responsibilities is a denial of the faith (1 Tim 5:8). Therefore, going to work, bringing home the earnings, and providing for your household in Christ's name bears fruit to God.

Furthermore, Scripture reveals that when couples fulfill their marriage vows and remain together, they are preserving a haven where they can raise the fruit that God is seeking—*godly offspring* (Mal 2:15).

8. Teaching Your Children in the Lord's Way

Similar to number seven above, we're fruitful when we teach our children in the ways of the Lord. In contrast, people in the world don't bear fruit to God because they don't teach their children the knowledge of God.

Parents are tasked with imparting God's word diligently to their children (Deut 6:6-7). Paul stressed the importance of fathers bringing up their children "in the training and admonition of the Lord" (Eph 6:4). Even if immediate results are not apparent, teaching our children about God's ways deposits something eternal in their souls. The promise holds: "Train up a child in the way he should go, and when he is old he will not depart from it" (Prov 22:6).

9. Enduring Persecution

When we suffer persecution for Christ's sake, He said we will enjoy the fruit of an eternal reward (Matt 5:10-12).

When the apostles suffered persecution, we're told they rejoiced at the privilege of suffering shame for His name (Acts 5:41). Why did they rejoice? Because they believed their sufferings gave glory to God and produced eternal fruit.

Same for us. When we suffer persecution for the cause of Christ, He remembers it forever and honors it with a great reward. That's true fruitfulness.

10. Glorifying God

Whenever we bring glory to God, we're storing up eternal fruit. Jesus pointed to this when He said, "By this My Father is glorified, that you bear much fruit; so you will be My disciples" (John 15:8).

In the context of that statement, Jesus was teaching on answered prayer. When we receive the things we desire in prayer, God is glorified. In other words, God is glorified through healings, miracles, deliverance, supernatural provision, healed relationships, etc. Jesus glorified the Father by healing many people, and now we glorify the Father the same way. When we're just like Jesus—performing signs and wonders—we demonstrate that we're His disciples and we glorify the Father.

To glorify God is to cause people's esteem of Him to elevate.

Let this be the consuming objective of all we do and say—to cause people's esteem of God to elevate. In a day when so many people curse the name of Jesus, let's do everything we can to help people esteem Christ more highly. When we do, we bear fruit to God.

Let me review the five examples given in this chapter. To be more fruitful, we seek to obey Jesus, provide security for our household, teach our children the knowledge of God, endure persecution, and glorify God.

When you review the ten ways to be fruitful mentioned in the previous and this chapter, you realize that fruitfulness is within reach. It's attainable for all of us!

Don't Be a Fruit Inspector

The ten examples of spiritual fruit listed in these two chapters are not supplied so we should look around, evaluate others, and determine whether they're fruitful. It's impossible for us to know how fruitful others are. Those we might consider to be extraordinarily fruitful may, in fact, be less fruitful than we realize; and those we might consider to be minimally fruitful may be evaluated differently by heaven. In fact, we're not even able to self-assess our own personal fruitfulness (1 Cor 4:3).

Paul wrote that we "bear fruit to God" (Rom 7:4). That means God alone knows how fruitful we are.

We might be able to recognize and measure someone else's *talents* to a certain degree (Matt 25:15), but we're not able to measure someone else's *fruitfulness*. We'll examine that distinction in the Appendix.

Therefore, let's not be fruit inspectors—trying to measure the fruitfulness of others. Instead, let's just concern ourselves with the garden of our own hearts, and keep reaching for ever-increasing fruitfulness

A Spectrum of Fruitfulness

In our parable, Jesus said, "But other seed fell on good ground and yielded a crop that sprang up, increased and produced: some thirtyfold, some sixty, and some a hundred" (Mark 4:8). What did Jesus mean by His designations of thirty, sixty, and a hundred?

He was speaking of *percentages*. Every disciple of Christ

is fruitful, in any particular season of life, at a percentage of their potential or calling. The Greek word used in verse 8 literally means, *up to thirty.* Jesus was acknowledging that fruitfulness happens across an entire spectrum of productivity.

The numbers thirty, sixty, and a hundred are not numbers to compare between two disciples. In other words, God doesn't compare you to your neighbor and say, "Next to your sister's fruitfulness, yours is only thirtyfold." Rather, thirty, sixty, and a hundred are measured against your own personal capacity and attainment. The numbers are given to encourage our own personal growth.

Nobody goes from thirtyfold to sixtyfold fruitfulness. Rather, we grow from thirtyfold to thirty-onefold. The journey is incremental, from glory to glory, and the goal is continuous progress toward our upward calling in Christ (Phil 3:14).

Jesus gave us the numbers thirty, sixty, and a hundred to incentivize us. Resident within the parable, therefore, is an invitation to grow. When we see that hundredfold fruitfulness is available to all of us, we're motivated to reach for more.

Here's what Paul wrote about his reach for hundredfold fruitfulness:

> **Not that I have already attained, or am already perfected; but I press on, that I may lay hold of that for which Christ Jesus has also laid hold of me. Brethren, I do not count myself to have apprehended; but one thing I do, forgetting those things which are behind and reaching forward to those things which are ahead, I press toward the goal for the prize of the upward call of God in Christ Jesus (Phil 3:12-14).**

Are you twenty-threefold fruitful? Reach for twenty-four. Are you seventy-fivefold fruitful? Reach for seventy-six. Keep reaching for the next level that's before you!

This concludes Part One, providing an introductory exploration of the parable. In Part Two, we'll delve deeper into Jesus' meaning when discussing the soil of the wayside. It's about to get good.

PART TWO

THE BIRDS

CHAPTER 9

The Birds

FOUR SOILS	HINDRANCE	MAIN ISSUE	CROP	TOOL
Trampled Heart	Birds	Unbelief	Stolen	Hoe
Shallow Heart	Stones	Tolerated Sin	Scorched	Shovel
Neglected Heart	Weeds	Distractions	Choked	Sickle
Fruitful Heart	All three	30/60/100-Fold	Productive	All three

Welcome to Part Two! In this section, we're going to launch our examination of the great question our parable raises:

Why aren't all Christians hundredfold fruitful?

Massive question! It stems from Jesus' words:

> **But these are the ones sown on good ground, those who hear the word, accept it, and bear fruit: some thirtyfold, some sixty, and some a hundred (Mark 4:20).**

Jesus indicated that believers differ in fruitfulness, identifying three levels: thirtyfold, sixty, and a hundred. We all *aspire* to be hundredfold fruitful, yet most of us realize we're still reaching for it.

What hinders believers from being hundredfold fruitful? And what can we do to overcome those hindrances? Those are the big questions we're going to excavate for the rest of this book. As answers are uncovered, the way of discipleship to Jesus will open before us in remarkable clarity.

We'll find that Jesus subtly embedded the answers *right inside the parable itself.*

Jesus will show us that, to obtain hundredfold fruitfulness, we must overcome three obstacles: birds, stones, and weeds. Our focus for the next six chapters will be on the first obstacle: the birds.

About Birds

Jesus made mention of the birds and what they represent:

> **And it happened, as he sowed, that some seed fell by the wayside; and the birds of the air came and devoured it (Mark 4:4).**
>
> **And these are the ones by the wayside where the word is sown. When they hear, Satan comes immediately and takes away the word that was sown in their hearts (Mark 4:15).**

According to Jesus, the birds symbolize Satan and, by association, the demons serving his evil purposes. Demons are on a relentless mission to steal the seed of God's word from anyone who hears it.

Every person reading this book is hassled by birds.

Birds love seeds. They live off seeds. If a demon can steal a seed that's been sown on your heart, it's energized. Nourished. Fueled. The seed that was meant to feed you instead feeds a demon.

The War for the Seed

A spiritual war takes place every time the word of God is heard or read. Anyone who spreads the word of God in any fashion should be savvy to this. Evangelists, take note—the birds are present every time you share the gospel with unbelievers. Preachers, be on alert—the birds are ready and waiting every time you preach the word to believers. They're hoping the hearts of some listeners won't believe your message. Why? Because when a listener's heart is hard, the seed bounces and just sits on the surface of the heart. Uncovered seeds are exactly what the demons are waiting for. They immediately descend and devour the exposed seeds. That person, in turn, goes their way and forgets the word they heard.

When an unbeliever's heart is completely hardened to the gospel, the birds will devour virtually all the seed sown on their heart. In contrast, when a believer with only partial hardness hears the word, the birds can get only some of their seed.

Every time you hear the word, you're warring with the birds. They're lurking right now, while you're reading this book. The war for the seed is real.

The Real Problem Is Not Birds

You can visualize Jesus' parable in your mind's eye, playing like a movie! You can imagine demons like hungry birds, flitting about, ready to dive and gobble any seed they can. When you visualize it this way, you quickly realize that the real problem here isn't the birds; the real problem is the condition of the heart. If the heart were soft, the seed would penetrate beyond the birds' reach.

The real problem is a hardened heart.

When soil is compacted hard, seeds can't gain entrance. And when a heart is compacted hard, the word of God can't penetrate the heart.

The Issue Is Unbelief

A hard heart responds to God's word with *unbelief.* Unbelief blocks the ability of the heart to open and receive the word.

You probably know what sunblock is. Well, unbelief is *wordblock*. Just as sunblock prevents UV rays from penetrating the skin, unbelief stops God's word from entering and warming the heart.

Some Christians mistakenly think that all they need to find is the right seed source. They suppose they're suffering from incompetent teachers who are serving up anemic seed. If only they could find the right teacher, or the right counselor, or the right mentor, or the right conference, or the right meeting, or the right online link, then they would be more fruitful.

But when your heart is hard, it doesn't matter how much seed you receive, none of it will penetrate.

You don't have a seed problem, you have a soil problem.[1]

A hard heart can seed-binge, but it still won't bear fruit. You can listen to the Bible on audiobook all day long, sing with your favorite worship playlists, and enjoy online messages from the most skillful Bible teachers, but as long as your heart is trampled hard, the seed won't penetrate.

Again, our real problem is not the demons that are hovering to steal our seed; our real problem is hardness of heart.

Hard Patches

Someone might wonder, *Can a Christian be fruitful in certain areas of their heart and still have patches of hardness in other places of their heart?*

According to Jesus, yes.[2]

For instance, on one occasion Jesus multiplied bread for five thousand men plus their families. Just a few hours later, the disciples were in a boat with Jesus and concerned that they had failed to bring enough bread with them. Already they had forgotten Jesus' ability to supply all their needs and more. In response, Jesus said to them, "Is your heart still hardened?" (Mark 8:17). The disciples were fruitful followers of Christ, yet there were still hard patches in their hearts.

---

1 Thanks to my friend Kelly Jenness for this sound bite.

2 For other verses where Jesus spoke of the hard hearts of His listeners, see Matthew 13:15; 19:8; Mark 3:5; 16:14; John 12:40.

When we, like the disciples, have hard patches in our hearts, we'll respond in faith when a word falls on a soft patch, but respond in unbelief when it falls on a hard patch. When a word falls on one of those hard patches, the birds will steal that seed from our hearts and diminish our fruitfulness.

Here's the good news, though. For disciples of Christ, the birds can't steal all your seed. Why not? Because your heart isn't entirely hardened. In places where your heart is permeable, God's word penetrates and the birds can't get to it. Those seeds will lodge in your heart, and you'll bear fruit to God.

By giving us this parable, Jesus was giving us a vision for targeting every hard patch of unbelief in our hearts. With His help, we're resolved to break up our hard patches and make them soft so every seed of God's word can find entrance.

When hearts are hard to the seed of God's word, His promises ring hollow, His will seems confining, obedience feels burdensome, and love is distant.

But when hearts are soft, His promises are obtainable, His will is delightful, obedience invigorates, and love flows freely.

How Do We Handle the Birds?

So, what can we do about those seed-stealing birds? First, here's something not to do. Don't concern yourself with scaring the birds off—because even if you do, they won't stay away for long.

For example, a preacher might pray, "Before I deliver this message, I take authority over every demon in this room that wants to steal the seed of God's word from the hearts of listeners. In Jesus' name, I command every bird to leave this room." Even if that prayer shooed away all the birds, the reprieve from their thievery would be very brief. In a quick minute, they'd all flit right back into the room and resume their mission of seed stealing.

In the parable, Jesus hinted at two responses that are

more effective in dealing with the birds:

- Minimize or eliminate things that trample your heart.
- Break up and soften the hardened parts of your heart.

To make this practical, I'm using the imagery of a hoe in this book to picture the breaking up our hard places (Jer 4:3). Just as a farmer swings a hoe into the ground to till it, we want to use a spiritual hoe to break up our fallow ground.

With hoe in hand, we're going to break up any hard places in our hearts and make them soft again. We don't use the hoe to scare away the birds, but to go after our hearts.

What can we do to minimize or eliminate the things that trample our hearts? For that question, keep reading.

CHAPTER 10

Trampled by People Traffic

In Jesus' parable, the wayside was hardened by foot traffic. Similarly, our hearts are hardened by everyday traffic that moves past our lives. What's the nature of that traffic? We're going to explore that question because, when we understand the things that trample our hearts, we can guard and foster a tender heart before God.

As a reminder, the wayside was a designated footpath that ran alongside a farmer's field. Farmers allowed pedestrians to walk the wayside, as long as they kept from wandering off and trampling the crops.

On the positive side, when travelers kept to the wayside, the crops were preserved. But on the negative side, the path itself became compacted and hard. Thus, when seed would fall on the wayside, it would bounce on the surface and immediately be devoured by birds.

This applies to our lives. Jesus likened our hearts to a field, with part of our hearts becoming trodden hard by foot traffic. When the seed of God's word lands on these hardened areas, rather than penetrating our hearts it bounces on the surface. Jesus said that demons, like birds, descend immediately and snatch that word from our hearts, causing us to forget the word we heard.

What would have trampled a wayside in Jesus' day? For starters, people and beasts. We're going to look at various kinds of foot traffic and how they apply to our lives. Let's begin with the first kind of foot traffic—people.

People Can Trample Your Heart

When people brush past our lives in the course of a day, they can trample our hearts with their words, attitudes, and actions. The only way to avoid this kind of trampling is to relocate to a remote wilderness somewhere and insulate yourself from all people contact. But if we do that, how can we possibly love our neighbor and make disciples as Jesus commanded? The only way to be a fruitful disciple is to live close to other people, but in so doing we make ourselves susceptible to their trampling.

Sometimes people trample us intentionally, but more often unintentionally. Either way, we can't stop or control their trampling; we can only control our responses.

Let's look at some of the ways people might trample our hearts.

Christians Can Trample Your Heart

For starters, other Christians can trample your heart. Maybe you assumed that mixing with other believers in the context of Christian community was a trample-free zone, but no. It seems odd to say it, but sometimes we can come away from times of Christian fellowship with our hearts made just a little bit harder because of the direction the conversation took. Just because the conversation was with another believer doesn't mean the word of faith was the only word on our tongues. It ought not to be so, but sometimes our tongues are set on fire by hell (see James 3:5-10). Sometimes we say things to other Christians that, instead of strengthening their faith, harden them to the word of faith.

Yes, other believers can trample our hearts with their words, attitudes, and actions. In fact, we can be especially vulnerable to trampling from other believers because we lower our guard when we're mixing with the family of faith. When they trample us, they don't even realize they're doing it, but we can come away from times of Christian fellowship with our hearts trampled just a little bit harder.

How did they trample us? Well, maybe they complained about their family, or their job, or their finances, or their health, or the decisions of church leaders, or the way God is silent to them right now, and their complaints trampled us. Or maybe they criticized, demeaned, or slandered other people in our presence. Slander will harden us *really* fast. Or they might vent their opinions on *disputable matters*. By disputable matters I mean issues where there's room in Christ for differences of opinion (see Rom 14:1, 5). Or they might volunteer advice that's based, not on the mind of Christ, but on their human understanding. They may relate in a way that makes us feel rejected or overlooked. They might defile us with the offense they carry toward someone else. They might talk about things that are meaningless and empty. They might draw carnal comparisons. In these and many other ways, other believers can harden our hearts.

I'm writing this chapter in the wake of the international COVID-19 upheaval of the 2020s. It was a time when believers had emotionally charged opinions about disputable matters. People left their churches in droves during that time of social upheaval. Sometimes it was because they had a problem with the way the pastor was responding to the COVID crisis. But some people left their church, not because they disagreed with their pastor, but with other people in the congregation. They didn't want to fellowship with believers who supported a certain political party or candidate. Political preferences became a source of division. When secular politics became the conversation within the church, hearts got trampled.

Additionally, pastors and church leaders got trampled in that season more than ever. For example, if leaders said people *should* wear face masks during church services, they got trampled by certain opinions in the church. Then, if leaders said people *shouldn't* wear face masks, they got trampled by other opinions in the church. Then, if leaders said everyone could decide for themselves about face masks, they got trampled by yet another set of opinions. It was virtually impossible for church leaders to make decisions in that season without getting trampled by *somebody*.

Pastors faced so many controversial choices that they came under decision fatigue. Should we meet indoors or outdoors? Should we practice social distancing? Should we obey or resist governmental restrictions? Almost every choice incurred some kind of pushback. Pastors were so trampled by Christians in that season that thousands left full-time vocational ministry.

This kind of trampling is not new to the church. It was happening in the time of Paul, who warned the Galatians, "But if you bite and devour one another, beware lest you be consumed by one another!" (Gal 5:15).

Yes, Christians can trample your heart.

Your Spouse Can Trample Your Heart

What's more, marriage can trample your heart. If you're married, that's probably not news to you. Like foot traffic that walked the wayside in Jesus' day, spouses can trample each other until both hearts are hard.

The most common way spouses trample each other is with their words. Unintentionally, your words can harden the heart of your spouse so that, when they hear the word of God, their response to God is dulled and diminished.

A husband tramples his wife with his words, and then she tramples him right back. Back and forth it goes. God intended marriage to edify and strengthen each other, but if we're not careful, it can be a context where we demean and devour one another.

Jesus addressed this. He said that, when believing couples divorce, it's because their hearts have become hard (Matt 19:8). He was describing a marriage in which two believers, married to each other, had so trampled each other that they lost faith for the marriage to be healed. Hardened in unbelief, they divorced.

A believer can have a soft heart in virtually every other area of their soul but, when it comes to their marriage, be hardened. They may love to worship and hear the word, they may weep with delight in their secret place, they may have excellent counsel for other believers, but when it comes to their own spouse, their heart is shut down and hardened with hopelessness.

If they're shown a Scripture that applies to marriage, they might dismiss it by saying, "Oh yes, I tried that." Or, "Tell that one to my spouse!" Or, "That verse doesn't apply in this case." When we're hardened, the word can bounce off our hearts like seeds on the wayside.

Trampling between spouses can sneak up on us. It might start as petty differences of opinion, but with time the arguments can heat up and the trampling can intensify. If we tolerate trampling in our marriage long enough, even skilled counselors might struggle to help us reverse the damage.

Sin Kills Marriages

When spouses trample each other, the problem—in a nutshell—is *sin*. When we pummel someone with our words, we're sinning against them (Gal 5:15). May I offer some marital advice?

Go after the sin in your marriage.

If you and your spouse are believers, resolve together by God's grace to get the sin out of your marriage—regardless of its nature. Zero tolerance for sin! Why? Because sin kills marriages.

Sin is a cancer. Tolerate sin in your home, and it'll gnaw at your marriage until it's dead.

On the other hand, if you'll put on the full armor of God and go after the sin in your home, your marriage will revive, your romance will be restored, and your home will heal. Christ has provided everything we need, through the cross, for our marriages to rebound and thrive (2 Peter 1:3).

I can suppose a brother asking, "What should I do if my wife sins against me?" Do what Jesus told you to do: "If your brother sins against you, rebuke him; and if he repents, forgive him" (Luke 17:3). If you're married to a sister in Christ and she sins against you, rebuke her. When she repents, forgive her. If she sins against you again, but then repents, forgive her again. Over and over.

I can suppose a sister asking the same question, "What should I do if my husband tramples me with his words, attitudes, or actions?" Do what Jesus said in Luke 17:3. When your believing husband sins against you, rebuke him. If you allow your brother in Christ—that is, your husband—to sin against you without rebuking him, you disobey Jesus.

Jesus said, "But why do you call Me 'Lord, Lord,' and not do the things which I say?" (Luke 6:46). Some Christian marriages are in disarray because they call Jesus their Lord, but don't do what He says—that is, they don't rebuke each other when their spouse sins against them.

If your spouse is an unbeliever, then your spouse is not your brother or sister in Christ and Luke 17:3 doesn't apply. In such cases, look for verses that guide our relationships with unbelievers, such as 1 Peter 3:1 and 1 Corinthians 7:12-16. But if your spouse is a believer and sins against you, don't sin by trampling them back; rather, rebuke them. Then step forward, together, into repentance and reconciliation. When you do, your heart can be healed and tender again to the implanted word.

People in the World Can Trample Your Heart

Interactions with non-believers can unintentionally harden our hearts. Their words proceed from an unbelieving heart, and words of unbelief trample a believing heart and desensitize us to the word of God.

Think of all the places where you interact with non-believers: work, school, sports, restaurants, stores, etc. Sometimes their words are idle, coarse, unkind, skeptical, proud, accusatory, critical, fearful, deceptive, boastful, or unloving, and their words can trample us.

Cultural values and institutions of a generation can also trample the hearts of a population. For example, young people go to university and get trampled all day, every day.

When people in the world harden us with their words or actions, what can we do to renew and soften our hearts? Consider this provision:

> **Let us draw near with a true heart in full assurance of faith, having our hearts sprinkled from an evil conscience and our bodies washed with pure water (Heb 10:22).**

When we've been defiled by unclean elements in the world, this verse mentions two things that cleanse and renew us: the sprinkled blood of Christ on our conscience, and the washing of the pure water of the word (Eph 5:26). The blood and the word provide the cleansing we need.

I find that I get defiled every day simply by living in this world. Therefore, I do two things every day: I receive by faith the sprinkled blood of Christ on my conscience,[1] and then I wash with water through the prayerful reading of Scripture. This is one way I use my spiritual hoe to soften my heart. (We'll talk in Chapter 13 about more ways to soften our hearts.)

---

1 The sprinkling of blood, as per Hebrews 10:22, is so precious to me that I've written an entire book on that subject. The title is *Power Of The Blood*, and it's available everywhere in both digital and paper formats.

The first kind of foot traffic, therefore, that can trample our hearts is people traffic. But there's more to say about this in the next chapter.

CHAPTER 11

Trampled by Family and Friends

Friends and family can also trample our hearts, simply because we spend so much time together. It seems unkind to say it so bluntly, but sometimes it's the people we love most who trample our hearts most.

We feel confident in the relationship, knowing we'll love each other regardless of what is said, so when we're together, we relax our guard and easily trample one another. We joke and laugh and have fun together, and can come away with our hearts hardened just a little bit more to the seed of God's word.

Hardened By Offense

Offense is a common way we're hardened by family and friends. When someone close to us offends us, and we harden ourselves a little bit toward that person, we harden simultaneously to the Lord. Then, when His word touches our hearts, it bounces on the surface. Satan loves when Christians are offended because they provide him with so many seed meals.

Nothing hardens the heart faster than offense.

We may think our offense is justified, but holding onto it produces all kinds of things that trample the heart—such as anger, resentment, unforgiveness, bitterness, or backbiting. The devil wants us to nurse the offense because he knows, even better than we do, how quickly offense will harden us and diminish our fruitfulness.

It's possible to be offended at someone even if they never actually wronged you. Judas Iscariot is an example of this. Jesus handled Judas perfectly, but Judas still got offended at Him (Mark 14:4, 10). Judas lost his soul because his heart was hardened by offense, and it led him to betrayal.

It's impossible for offended Christians to grow in fruitfulness.

Someone might promise themselves, *I'm never going to let them hurt me like that again.* But when we harden ourselves to other people, we harden simultaneously to the seed of God's word.

Offended people sometimes become the hero of their own narrative. They think they see a speck in someone else's eye, but are blind to the beam in their own eye (Matt 7:3-5). Beware the hardness that comes with offense—it can jade our perceptions and blind us to our own sin.

Abuse

Abuse hardens the heart. Friends and family can harden us through things like physical and emotional abuse, molestation, violation, and exploitation. Some who were violated in their youth still have a place of painful hardness in their heart, even many years later.

Jesus issued one of His strongest warnings to those who offend children (Matt 18:6-7). When a child's heart is trampled by trauma, it can be challenging for them even in adulthood to receive the seed of God's word.

Stop for a moment and reflect on your childhood. When you were young and vulnerable, did someone close to you sin against you and trample your heart? If so, then I invite you to get out your spiritual hoe and decide, before God, that you're going to go after that hard patch in your heart.

That person could harden your heart, but they can't soften it. Only you can soften your heart, with the help of the Holy Spirit.

You may not know right now how to break up that hardened ground in your heart, but resolve by God's grace that you're going after it. You may want to pray, *Lord, I'm not going to relent until You show me how to use my hoe and break up that hard patch in my heart.*

This may mean some spiritual violence on your part. Go ahead, go after your heart! Jesus referred to this when He said, "The kingdom of heaven suffers violence, and the violent take it by force" (Matt 11:12). Use every means at your disposal, whether wise counsel from others, a scriptural study, fasting, or receiving anointing with oil and prayer (James 5:14), etc. Wield your hoe with the Lord's strength and go after the hardness until your heart is tender in that area.

Paranoia can be a symptom of a trampled heart. When a part of our heart has been trampled repeatedly by people, we can become paranoid about when the next hit will come. If you've been trampled repeatedly by someone in the same place of your heart, now you've got some spiritual work to do. Get out your hoe and go after that hard patch until it's soft to the seed of God's word.

Hardened By Rejection

Rejection can trample the heart. Rejection from family and friends can be especially trampling because of how close they are to us.

Probably every reader of this book has been rejected by a friend or family member sometime in life. Why would I say that? Because rejection is a universal human experience. It's impossible to live on this planet without eventually encountering rejection in the journey. How we respond is very important, however, because our response profoundly affects the fruitfulness of our lives.

For a fantastic example of that statement, read the story of Joseph. His brothers rejected him in a deep way, selling him into slavery and making money off his distress. But Joseph saw God's hand in his trial, responded with forgiveness, and made his way forward to hundredfold fruitfulness.

Rejection can take many forms. People can slander, criticize, ostracize, accuse, disown, shun, scold, despise, judge, hate, or discriminate against you. Maybe you did something to trigger their rejection, or maybe you didn't. Either way, rejection tramples the heart.

Rejection is a complex topic, so much so that I've written a separate book, *Dealing With the Rejection and Praise of Man.* In it, I wrote that rejection is one of God's specialty tools that He uses to form those He especially likes. For example, Joseph would have never become the great man he was without the rejection of his brothers. Almost all the heroes of the Bible were formed by God through the tool of rejection.

Our greatest Hero of all, Jesus Christ, experienced uncommon rejection during His earthly ministry—especially from the tenured leaders of His day. He was betrayed by one of His most intimate associates, and then the frothing bulls ran at Him, gored, and crucified Him. When people hate you enough to kill you, you can rightly call it rejection.

It's stunning to consider that Jesus never hardened to His murderers. We see His softness in the way He related to Judas Iscariot. Knowing that Judas was about to betray Him, Jesus took a towel in hand and, with a basin of water, tenderly washed Judas' feet (see John 13:2-5). Jesus showed love and care, even though Judas had already arranged with the Jewish leaders to betray Him. Jesus refused to allow Judas' trampling to harden His heart.

Jesus' example shows us what to do when family or friends reject us: We'll wash their feet. We probably won't wash their feet *literally* with soap and water, but we'll wash their feet *figuratively* by doing something that refreshes, relieves, rejuvenates, or helps them. In so doing, we're using a hoe on our hearts. Like Jesus, we're refusing to allow their rejection to harden us.

When someone rejects you, therefore, ask the Lord,

"What can I do to refresh or bless this person?" When you do what the Lord shows you, you'll wash that person's feet and you'll keep your own heart soft and receptive to the seed of God's word.

Softened through Forgiveness

When we've been trampled by family or friends, one of the ways we brandish our hoe and break up our fallow ground is through forgiveness. Forgiveness restores a soft heart, and opens us to the seed of God's word. Disciples of Jesus pursue forgiveness aggressively, therefore, because we know how pivotal it is to becoming more fruitful.

I want to say ten things about forgiveness.

1. Jesus taught on forgiveness repeatedly. It's the only option for disciples of Christ (see Luke 17:3).

2. Forgiveness is a choice. When Jesus taught on it, He never told us *how* to forgive, He just told us to do it (Matt 6:12-15). His simple directive seemed to imply we have the power, by His grace, to do it.

3. Forgiveness is something we do over and over. When Jesus talked about forgiveness, He said it's something we do "up to seventy times seven" (Matt 18:22). When someone has wronged you, therefore, forgive them again and again. When you feel unforgiveness trying to creep back in and harden your heart, forgive all over again. Repeat until all vestiges of unforgiveness are gone.

4. Jesus indicated unforgiveness comes with torment (Matt 18:32-34). Unforgiveness only hurts ourselves. As the saying goes, to refuse to forgive is like drinking poison and expecting the other person to die.

5. We forgive others because they don't know what they do (see Luke 23:34). They don't know they're trampling our hearts.

6. When we forgive others, then we can receive forgiveness ourselves from God (see Matt 5:7). We forgive because we desperately need to be forgiven.

7. When a wrong has been committed, someone must pay the price of punishment. According to Tim Keller, when we forgive the wrong someone has committed against us, we're absorbing the punishment and paying the price for what was done against us.[1] Thus, forgiveness is costly and precious.

8. We forgive whether or not the other person apologizes or acknowledges wrongdoing.

9. We forgive others because God has forgiven us. Nobody has offended us more than we've offended God.

10. Forgiveness asks that God not judge that person at the last day for the sin they committed against us. Thus, forgiveness prays, "Lord, do not charge them with this sin" (Acts 7:60). After all, that person probably has enough sin already on their account. When we forgive someone, God expunges that infraction from heaven's records. Forgiveness, therefore, is forever.

You may want to pause here and pray, *Lord, I renew my resolve to forgive everyone who sins against me. Give me the grace to forgive completely, and may bitterness or offence never be able to harden my heart. I receive Your help—thank You for a soft heart!*

---

1 From a Tim Keller podcast, episode unknown.

In a couple chapters, we're going to look at more ways to use our hoe and soften our hearts. But before we get to that, there's more to be said about the various ways our hearts can be trampled.

CHAPTER 12

Trampled by Beasts

We've said people can trample our hearts, but there's another kind of foot traffic that can also leave us trampled —beasts.

In ancient times, livestock owners guided their animals—donkeys, mules, camels, sheep, oxen, cows, horses, or goats—along footpaths to reach their destination. After all, it was both people and beasts that needed a path past the farmer's field. Entire herds of cattle and flocks of sheep were moved in this fashion via the wayside, trampling it even further.

The animal traffic of Jesus' day represents the beasts of unbelief that can trample our hearts today.

The term *beasts of unbelief* derives from putting Psalms 14 and 73 together. Psalm 14:1 says unbelief is foolish. When the psalmist was gripped by the foolishness of unbelief, he wrote, "I was like a beast before You" (Ps 73:22). Foolish unbelief had so hardened his heart that he was like a beast before God. He was saying his unbelief was beastly.

Unbelief is beastly.

Every culture has beastly influences that roam the paths of society and promote unbelief. When we walk the concourses of society, our hearts inescapably get trampled by beastly influences that harden our hearts. When we're trampled by these beasts, our hearts harden just a little bit more, and our ability to receive every seed of God's word is diminished.

What Are the Beasts?

Some of the cultural beasts we have in the United States include media and streaming services such as ABC, NBC, CBS, FOX, CNN, HBO, Univision, Netflix, Hulu, Discovery

Plus, Apple TV, Disney, YouTube, Amazon Prime, Peacock, TikTok, Facebook, Instagram, Google, Audible, Kindle, podcasts, novels, magazines, radio, etc.

When you watch a news anchor on a news outlet such as CNN or FOX, set a guard around your heart because you're likely to get trampled.

When you allow yourself to watch a movie, you might want to brace yourself because your heart is probably going to get trampled. The rating on the movie—whether PG, PG13, or R—simply indicates the degree to which your heart will be trampled.

Many shows blaspheme Jesus' beautiful name or contain violence, sexual content, or expletives. When we consume this kind of content, our hearts get trampled.

Some of us have been so hardened by beasts that, when we're trampled again, it doesn't bother us anymore.

Today's creators of beastly entertainment are extremely clever at their craft. I've experienced their skill at pulling us into their intriguing plots. More than once, I've been drawn to a movie because of the creative plot and riveting cinematography. I'll keep watching because I think the storyline has potential to become very entertaining. (I'm a bit of a sucker for suspenseful hero stories filled with mystery and intrigue.) What I don't always realize, until later, is that I'm being trampled.

For example, I remember waking up one morning and realizing that the movie I had watched the night before had trampled my heart. I didn't realize it while watching the movie, but I had allowed beasts of movie violence to stomp on me. It took me several hours, on that occasion, to recover tenderness in my heart.

I've decided that no film is so entertaining that it's worth the hardening of my heart.

There are other beasts of culture, beyond just media platforms. A friend observed that we can also be trampled by cultural standards of beauty, prompting people to get surgery to beautify their features. Cultural values on gender identity can trample us, as can political values. Our culture is full of beasts.

A Soft Heart Is a Delicate Thing

Here's a key difference between people traffic and animal traffic. We can't stop people from trampling us because we can't control what they might do or say. But with beasts it's different. We have the ability to control what the beasts might do to us. When the beasts of our culture trample us, it's usually because we've allowed them access.

Somebody reading my earlier comments about movie violence might think I sound a bit religious, legalistic, or stodgy. But for me, the issue isn't inflexibility, it's influence. You see, I'm pursuing mountain-moving faith. I'm pursuing kingdom authority and Spirit-filled faith to heal the sick and raise the dead. I don't need sources of entertainment, therefore, that harden me to Holy Spirit possibilities. More than anything in the world, I need a soft heart that opens readily to seeds of faith. Faith is a delicate thing and is easily forfeited. As Rees Howells said, "Take care you are believing. Believing is the most delicate thing you can think of. It is like a vapor; you can easily miss it."[1] Faith is like a tender plant that's easy to kill. Traffic can trample it, stones can wither it, and weeds can choke it. We must be vigilant to guard our hearts if we're to apprehend mountain-moving faith (Prov 4:23; 1 Tim 6:12).

Depression

I'm including depression in this chapter because I view it mostly as a wayside problem. But in this case, depression is caused by beasts we *can't* control. Depression is often

---

1 Norman Grubb, *Rees Howells, Intercessor* (Fort Washington, PA: CLC Publications, 2001) 244.

triggered by beastly circumstances beyond our control that trample us really hard. Then our emotions start to escalate, overwhelming our souls with feelings of helplessness and hopelessness. Thoughts of unbelief roar in our ears, *You will never recover from this!*

The fight with depression is called, in the Bible, the fight of faith (1 Tim 6:12). Depression tries to gut our faith. In response, soldiers of faith get in the fight to recover their confidence in God. When depression trumpets its lies, the soldier fights for every fiery dart to be quenched and for faith to prevail (Eph 6:16).

Why, when we're battling depression, do we sometimes turn to the beasts of our culture for comfort? As though NetFlix could buoy our souls. Instead, our hearts just get trampled even more.

If you're depressed and fighting to breathe, turn to the word of God not the beasts. Fight! Work your heart, labor in the word, and stay at it—no matter how long—until your heart is soft and receiving once again the word of faith.

To recap, we've talked about trampling from people traffic and animal traffic. But I wonder if there might be a third way our hearts can be trampled. I'm wondering—is it possible that our hearts can be trampled by the footsteps of the Sower Himself?

The Sower Walked the Wayside

Jesus is the Sower, and at first glance it seems inconceivable to suppose that Jesus might trample a believer's heart. But still, I'm going to ask the question. Could our hearts possibly be trampled by the Sower?

I'm asking because the sower in the parable would have used the wayside as a footpath to get from one quadrant of his field to another. Could we conclude, therefore, that the sower's feet also contributed to the wayside's hardening? Is it possible that our hearts could be trampled by the way Jesus chooses to walk with us?

Without question, Jesus has a unique walk. Sometimes He walks in ways we don't anticipate or understand. When His feet lead us in paths we don't enjoy, we can respond wrongly to His leadership and come away with a hardened heart.

Think for a moment about His unique walk. Sometimes He waits when we want immediate answers. Sometimes He restrains Himself when we want Him to act decisively. Sometimes He tests us when we don't think we need it. Sometimes He prunes when we think we're being really fruitful. Sometimes He rebukes and chastens when we're totally sincere and giving Him our biggest *yes* (Rev 3:19).

When you're John the Baptist—the Bridegroom's best friend—suffering in prison, and Jesus does nothing to get you out even though He's anointed to open prison doors, it's tempting to be offended and hardened by Him (see Isa 61:1; Matt 11:6; John 3:29).

Jesus has His own cadence and stride, and even though we follow His steps with sincerity and zeal, the course of the journey sometimes disappoints and makes us heartsick (Prov 13:12). When He delays the answers to our prayers, we can be tempted to lose heart and become weary.

Have you ever met a believer who was angry at God? Have you known anyone who struggled with being offended at Jesus for the way He was walking with them through life? Would it be appropriate to say their heart was trampled by the Sower—or, to be more precise, trampled by their misunderstanding of His perfect leadership?

When someone's heart is being trampled by divinely orchestrated circumstances, the adversary is right there to accuse the Sower's intentions. The accuser wants us to be ungrateful for the path Jesus has us on. He wants us to partner with his accusations against God. The accuser wants us thinking, *This isn't right. God isn't fulfilling His promises in my life. I've been faithful to Him, but He's not being faithful to me. The way He's walking with me is unloving, unkind, and unfair.*

Job was a man in the Bible who struggled with the way God walked with him in his journey. He wrote,

> **My foot has held fast to His steps; I have kept His way and not turned aside. I have not departed from the commandment of His lips; I have treasured the words of His mouth more than my necessary food. But He is unique, and who can make Him change? And whatever His soul desires, that He does (Job 23:11-13).**

Job held to his Master's steps but found that the Sower is *unique*. He has a way of walking that is different from all others. He'll never change but insists that we always change. When we feel trampled by the way He's walking with us, we're the ones who must change.

Was Judas Iscariot Trampled by the Sower?

From my vantage, it seems that Judas was trampled by the way Jesus walked with him. I'm thinking of the time Judas rebuked Mary for pouring her expensive oil on Jesus (John 12:4-5). In response, Jesus rebuked Judas for criticizing Mary's extravagance. Judas had rebuked Mary publicly, so Jesus responded in kind and rebuked Judas publicly (John 12:7-8).

Judas probably felt shamed and humiliated. I wonder if he was possibly thinking, *I can never say anything right. Nothing I do or say is ever good enough for Jesus. I'll never be in the inner circle. I need to get in reality and recognize that I don't have a future on His team.*

Judas' public humiliation seemed to be the final straw. It seemed to harden his heart finally and completely to Jesus.

Jesus' rebuke forced Judas toward a decision. Either the rebuke would help him or harden him. In this case, Judas took Jesus' rebuke as a trampling.

Judas' hardened heart caused him to respond in a tragic way. It's possible he was thinking something like, *It's time for me to leave Jesus' team, but if I do it strategically, I think I can make this a win-win for both of us. I see a way to exit the team with a sweet wad of cash and at the same time set Jesus up so He can reveal Himself and come into His own.*

It seems Judas didn't expect Jesus to be arrested and condemned (see Matt 27:3). After all, Jesus had always averted every attempted arrest. It seems that Judas expected Jesus to escape as He had so many times before. Judas probably thought he was helping with Jesus' unveiling. It wasn't until he saw Jesus was condemned that Judas realized the tragedy of his betrayal.

Even though Jesus walked perfectly with Judas, Judas' heart still got hardened. It seems he was trampled by the Sower.

What should we do when we don't enjoy the way Jesus is walking with us? Like Job, choose to worship (Job 1:20). Praise the Sower for His *perfect* stride! Set your love on Him (Ps 91:14). Surrender and submit to Him. Worship Him for His brilliant leadership in your life. Above all, keep your heart soft to Him.

When we guard a soft heart, we will continue to walk forward into greater fruitfulness in Christ.

CHAPTER 13

How Can We Soften Our Hearts?

All of us know what it's like for our heart to be hard and resistant to God's word because all of us have been trampled by people and by beasts of culture. When the seed can't penetrate our unbelief, it bounces on the surface of our hearts, is devoured by demons, and then forgotten.

What can we do about hardened places in our hearts? The prophets called on us to break up the fallow ground of our hearts:

> **"Break up your fallow ground"** (Jer 4:3).
>
> **Sow for yourselves righteousness; reap in mercy; break up your fallow ground, for it is time to seek the LORD, till He comes and rains righteousness on you (Hos 10:12).**
>
> **So rend your heart, and not your garments (Joel 2:12-13).**

People and beasts can harden us, but only we can soften our hearts by breaking up our fallow ground.

What is fallow ground? Untended soil that has the potential to produce a crop but has been left uncultivated for a while. Consequently, fallow ground is hard, neglected, and barren.

Before fallow ground can be seeded, it must be tilled or plowed. Gardeners use a variety of instruments for this purpose, but my tool of choice to illustrate this task is a farmer's *hoe*.

Get Out Your Hoe

A farmer uses a hoe to break up hardened soil by driving the hoe vigorously into the ground. That action illustrates, in a way, how we soften our hearts before God. We swing the implements God has given us in His word to break up the hard places of our hearts.

Envision this in your mind's eye. Picture yourself taking a garden hoe in hand, positioning it with the sharp corner forward, lifting it high above your head, bringing it down with all your strength, and driving it as deeply as you can into the soil. Over and over. The work is rigorous, but you've got a job to do and you're going after it. That picture illustrates what you're doing to your heart. With your spiritual hoe in hand, you're using spiritual violence to break up the fallow ground of your heart. With each blow, your heart keeps getting softer and more receptive to seed.

That's how aggressive Jesus wants us to be with the hard places of our hearts.

Exercise strength, focus, and persistence. Stay with it until the entirety of your heart is soft and receptive to the word of faith.

The very fact that God called us, through the prophets, to break up our fallow ground indicates that He's present to help us. He will give us grace for this task!

But how do we do this? How do we swing our hoe and soften our hearts? Let me suggest seven practical ways we can break up the fallow ground of our hearts.

Repent

To repent means two things: to turn away, and to turn toward. We turn away from our sins, and we turn toward God.

God loves a contrite spirit (Isa 66:2). A contrite heart is quick to agree with God about its sins and shortcomings. When the Holy Spirit convicts us of sin, a contrite spirit doesn't argue with God and defend itself. Rather, it says, "Yes, Lord, You're right! I've been sinning in that area, and I'm troubled by it. It's wrong, and I'm confessing it. Please forgive me and help me to change."

When we're repenting of sin, we're using our hoe and breaking up hard places in our hearts. Plowing is the hardest work of a farmer's year, and the same will probably be true for us. True repentance is hard work. Getting our hearts soft sometimes means getting our knees hard.

Repentance is hard work because it's more than just feeling sorry for our sin; it's resolving, by God's grace, to change and stop sinning. God has more than enough grace to help us overcome, but we must access it through wholehearted repentance and faith.

Hear the call of Jesus, "Therefore be zealous and repent" (Rev 3:19). Just as a farmer swings his hoe strenuously to break up the soil, be zealous to repent. Make room for new seed.

On one occasion, Jesus talked about a man who dug deep in order to lay the foundation of his house on subterranean rock (Luke 6:48). A contrite heart, therefore, digs deep. Swing your hoe of repentance, go deep, and break up the hard places of your heart. When you do, you make a way for greater fruitfulness.

Weep

Weeping is one of the most beautiful ways to soften our hearts before God. When we're in anguish over our hardness and long for His help to overcome our unbelief, tears can sometimes flow. Tears wash the heart and make it easier for the hoe to penetrate.

We weep because we mourn. We mourn the way our hard hearts have resisted the seed of God's word. We mourn our unbelief. He called us to mourn in this way:

> **"Now, therefore," says the LORD, "Turn to Me with all your heart, with fasting, with weeping, and with mourning." So rend your heart, and not your garments; return to the LORD your God, for He is gracious and merciful, slow to anger, and of great kindness; and He relents from doing harm (Joel 2:12-13).**

Do you have any idea how many things you've lost because of unbelief? When the Holy Spirit reveals the losses your unbelief has cost you, you'll mourn. Weeping and mourning are sweet gifts from above to soften the heart.

When you see a hard place in your heart, but don't know how to treat it, sometimes the only thing you can do is mourn it. As you mourn your hardness, cling to Jesus' promise, "Blessed are those who mourn, for they shall be comforted" (Matt 5:4). Mourn the things you can't change in your own power. When you mourn your unbelief, God comforts you by softening your heart and strengthening your faith.

Don't resist tears. Rather, ask for the gift of tears. Tears are liquid love. They express things words never could. Tears are louder to God than tongues. They're so precious to Him that He collects and bottles them (Ps 56:8).

We're not trying to *manufacture* tears. God isn't moved by pretenses. Contrived tears soften nothing. But when tears are authentic and wholehearted, they have a remarkable way of softening the heart.

Forgive

Thirdly, we soften our hearts by forgiving those who have sinned against us. Just as unforgiveness hardens the heart, forgiveness softens it.

Pray by name for the people who have given you trouble. Ask the Lord to be merciful to them and to you.

You may want to revisit the end of Chapter Eleven, where we talked about forgiveness, because we won't repeat those comments here. But suffice it to say, when we're forgiving others, we're swinging our hoe and softening our hearts.

Fast

If you want to soften your heart, consider fasting. Fasting is a sublime gift from God! It's virtually unparalleled in its ability to soften the heart.

Fasting, prayer, and word immersion have literally saved my life. I would have been a spiritual casualty in my journey were it not for these gifts. Oh, that the Lord would grace my pen to commend you to the wisdom and grace of fasting.

I advise every disciple of Jesus to do an annual ten-day water-only fast. First off, here's why I recommend water only. The primary purpose of fasting is to increase the intensity of your pursuit after Jesus. If you're going to do that, why take the edge off by dulling it with calories? Go all in and do water only. Go hard after Jesus!

And secondly, I recommend ten days because of the threshold that is crossed around day seven. Let me explain.

On a water fast, I've found day two to be the toughest. If you can survive day two, you can make it the whole way. In my opinion, the purpose of day two on a water-only fast is to get to day three, smile. On day three, you start the slow journey of emerging from the fog. Each day thereafter gets increasingly clearer.

Right around day seven, you break free of the surf line. What I mean is, you cross a threshold where the turbulence of the surf line gets behind you, and you move out into the smooth sailing of the open waters. Your body starts to cooperate with you, and the fast gets easier. This is where some of your best revitalization may happen. Once you get there, why not enjoy it for three more days? Do ten days!

If you're not able to do a water-only fast because of health restrictions, then get as close to it as you safely can (under medical advisement). If the prospect of a ten-day fast is too daunting, start small and work your way up.

When on a water-only fast, muscle down your schedule to minimize distractions and devote yourself as fully as possible to the word and prayer. If you need to meet performance expectations on your job, don't do a water-only fast. Save it for a time when you can get away with Jesus.

If you should follow my advice and do a ten-day water-only fast—because of your sincere longing for more of Jesus—then I promise: It *will* soften your heart.

Pray the Scriptures

Praying from Scripture is one of our greatest delights and sweetest disciplines. When I speak of praying from Scripture, I mean the beautiful practice of using the language of a verse to have an extended conversation with Jesus.

How do we pray a verse? In every conceivable way possible. Pull on it, push on it, pray it from every direction, squeeze it, wring it out, put pressure on it, and excavate it. Pray the verse until your heart is captured by it and faith springs alive.

When you pray from Scripture, it puts chutzpah into your prayer life because you know you're praying according to the will of God. What's more, you never run out of stuff to talk to God about because Scripture supplies an inexhaustible treasure trove of holy prayer fodder.

When I'm praying a Scripture, I'm working and massaging the seeds of that verse deeper into the soil of my heart. Or, to be more accurate, I'm turning over the soil of my heart so that the seed of the word can gain greater entrance. As I pray a verse, I listen for what Jesus might say to me through that verse because I know that faith comes by hearing (Rom 10:17).

Take it from an old guy with some experience: Praying the word softens the heart.

Erect Guardrails

If you want to keep your heart soft, set up traffic guardrails to protect your heart from trampling. In other words, establish limits around your heart so that the beasts of our culture can't get to the garden of your heart. Refuse the beasts access and your heart will be less trampled.

Let me suggest a couple ways we might shield our hearts from the hooves of beasts. Regarding porn, we can make a covenant with our eyes (see Job 31:1).[1] Regarding movies, we can resolve that we're not going to watch movies with certain ungodly content. Regarding social media, we might limit the amount of time spent daily on apps and sites. Regarding video streaming, we might limit the number of streaming services we use and the kinds of programs we allow.

Serve notice to the beasts that want to trample your heart by metaphorically placing No Trespassing signs around your heart. *This far and no further.*

If you're careful to put wise guardrails around your heart, I assure you that your heart will remain softer and more permeable to the seed of God's word.

O Lord, give us a vision for cultivating and keeping a soft heart!

Get Wet

When it comes to keeping your heart soft, I want to mention a final ingredient that's absolutely essential to soft soil: *Rain.*

In the land of Israel, fields get baked hard under the sizzling summer sun. Somewhere between October and

---

1 See my book, *A Covenant With My Eyes.*

December, the *early rains* (also called the *former rain*) typically arrive. Farmers waited to plow their fields until the early rains arrived because, until the soil was softened by rain, it would be virtually impossible to break up the hard-baked soil. Rain made the soil supple so that a plow could break it up. In the fall, even if a farmer was really eager to plow his fields, he was helpless to begin until the early rains fell. Without rain, plowing was impossible.

Similarly, we can break up the fallow ground of our hardened hearts only with the enabling rain of the Holy Spirit.[2] The rain doesn't plow our hearts—that's work we must do—but it does make our hearts pliable and makes plowing possible.

If you need the rain of the Holy Spirit on your hard heart, ask for it. The Scripture says, "Ask the LORD for rain" (Zech 10:1). To those who ask, He extends this promise: "He will come to us like the rain, like the latter and former rain to the earth" (Hos 6:3). If you ask, He will come.

Holy Spirit, rain on me! Help me to soften my heart! As you pray, open your heart and receive the refreshing waters of the Holy Spirit. He will help you.

In summary, we've looked at seven ways we can take our hoe in hand and soften our hearts:

Repent.
Weep.
Forgive.
Fast.
Pray Scripture.
Erect guardrails.
Ask for rain.

---

2 I'm likening the Holy Spirit's ministry to rain because Jesus said, in John 7:38-39, that the Holy Spirit flows within us like rivers of living water. See also Joel 2:28-29.

This is the end of Part Two—our treatment of the birds and the wayside soil. Part Three will look carefully at the stones of compromise that hinder our fruitfulness. Here we go!

PART THREE

THE STONES

CHAPTER 14

The Stones

FOUR SOILS	HINDRANCE	MAIN ISSUE	CROP	TOOL
Trampled Heart	Birds	Unbelief	Stolen	Hoe
Shallow Heart	Stones	Tolerated Sin	Scorched	Shovel
Neglected Heart	Weeds	Distractions	Choked	Sickle
Fruitful Heart	All three	30/60/100-Fold	Productive	All three

Welcome to Part Three! In this section, we're tackling the problem of stones in the garden of our heart.

Jesus said three things hinder us from hundredfold fruitfulness: birds, stones, and weeds (see the above chart). The measure of our victory over these three determines the measure of our fruitfulness.

A thirtyfold fruitful disciple is someone who is *somewhat* victorious over the birds, stones, and weeds. A sixtyfold fruitful disciple is someone who is *significantly* victorious over the birds, stones, and weeds. And a hundredfold fruitful disciple is someone who is *completely* victorious over those three hindrances. They're truly an overcomer!

In the previous chapters, we talked about how we overcome the birds. Now, let's look at how disciples gain victory over stones.

In the parable, Jesus talked about stones in a garden that diminish the strength of a crop. *Those stones represent pockets of sin or compromise that hinder our root development.*

Stones diminish crops, so wise gardeners never tolerate them. When they find a stone, they dig it up and remove it. In this book, we're using a shovel to represent how we remove stones from our hearts. When we find a stone in our hearts, we dig with our spiritual shovel and remove the stone from our hearts.

Stones Hide

Stones often hide below the surface of a garden, out of view. Every one of us, therefore, probably has stones in the garden of our heart that we don't know are still there. In other words, there are pockets of sin in our hearts that we haven't yet identified.

As we walk with Christ, He takes us on a journey of revealing the stones in our heart. When we see them, then we can deal with them and remove them from our garden. If you've been in the faith for a while, you've probably recognized many stones of compromise through the years and gotten rid of them. But it's likely there are still others remaining—stones of compromise in your heart that you still haven't seen.

We're encouraged in the journey, however, because we have fewer stones today than yesterday! Our hearts are becoming increasingly free of stones and we're growing in fruitfulness.

Surprise!

Stones will surprise you. If you've done any gardening, you've probably been surprised by stones, especially when it's time to break up and aerate the soil of your garden. You push your spade into the ground and feel a sudden *thud*. The shovel stops and won't penetrate deeper. *A stone!* You might even wonder, *Where did that stone come from? It wasn't there last year! Who put it there?* Virtually every gardener knows what it's like to hit, by surprise, into a stone.

Why would a stone suddenly appear in your garden?

Answer: *change of seasons.* When temperatures fluctuate and precipitation increases, stones that were buried in the ground can slowly work their way toward the surface. These movements are even more noticeable in climates where the ground freezes in winter. For example, in the cold northeast of the US, the sudden appearance of stones in gardens is so common that they're sometimes called *New England potatoes.*

When a stone surfaces in your yard that you hadn't spotted before, it was actually in the ground all along. It just needed enough seasonal changes to work its way toward the surface until it came into view.

A similar dynamic can happen in our lives spiritually. We can be walking forward cheerfully with the Lord when, all of a sudden, we come across a stone of compromise in our heart we didn't know was there. We look to our left and right and wonder, *Who put that stone in the garden of my heart?* No one, of course. That pocket of compromise was in our heart all along—deep, hidden, unidentified. It probably surfaced because of a change of season. Seasonal changes can reveal things that were hidden in our hearts all along.

What exactly do we mean by a *change of spiritual seasons?* Just as the four seasons naturally change around us, our walk with God also goes through cyclical seasons. Some seasons are harder, or dryer, or happier, or more fruitful than others. Seasons often change with a change of circumstances. The new circumstances might feel positive, but in many cases a change of season is associated with something disruptive or uncomfortable. The change might be connected to our family, or a promotion, or a change of address, or an unexpected event, or a new challenge, or an accident, or a fresh encounter with God. When our season changes, iniquities that were hidden in our hearts can suddenly surface.

On the one hand, new circumstances can be emotionally challenging to navigate; but they can also be encouraging when we realize God is using them to surface things in our hearts that really need to be addressed. Without the changes, you wouldn't have seen that stone of compromise in your heart. But now that you see it, you can remove it and step into even greater fruitfulness. The stormy change of seasons was actually a kindness!

Decision Time

When your spade locates a stone in your garden, you face a decision. You can postpone dealing with it, or you can stop and do what's necessary to dig it up and toss it.

Sometimes it's tempting, in the moment, to procrastinate its eviction. Maybe we're in a hurry, or maybe we're a little bit lazy, or maybe we just don't want to let go of that carnal indulgence just yet. But here's what Jesus wants us to see in His parable: If we tolerate or overlook a stone of compromise that He's showing us, that stone is *guaranteed* to hinder the fruitfulness of our heart. To be more fruitful disciples of Christ, we must stop and go after it.

Stones can take more work to remove than you were expecting. I experienced this once with a certain stone in my lawn. The stone was getting more and more exposed above the grass, and I knew that one of these days my lawnmower blade was going to hit it. A moment came when I decided, *It's time for this stone to go.* So I grabbed my shovel and began to attack the thing. The more I dug, the bigger the stone got. I had no idea how huge that stone would turn out to be. It took nearly an hour to finish the job. What I thought was a stone turned out to be a *boulder.*

Here's what I gleaned from that experience: I shouldn't be surprised if removing a certain sin from my life ends up being a more rigorous task than initially expected. Nor should I be daunted or deterred from the mission. I won't relax, procrastinate, lose heart, or quit. I'm going to go after the nasty critter until it's fully removed from my heart.

If we'll go after our stones with that kind of tenacious resolve, we will most assuredly become more fruitful disciples of Christ!

Zero Toleration

Decide right now, even before we talk about specific kinds of stones, that you're never going to tolerate any stones of compromise that God shows you. Resolve that whenever you see a stone in your heart, you're going to go after it until it's pulled up and discarded.

Sometimes we're tempted to medicate our stones. What I mean is, when we see a pocket of sin in our hearts, instead of digging it up and removing it, we can be tempted to medicate it. People medicate their stones with things like prescription drugs, illegal drugs, alcohol, shopping, pleasures, etc. Self-medicating doesn't get rid of our stones, it only masks their presence so they don't trouble us as much. Refuse to medicate your stones. Go the route of repentance and *remove* your stones.

Tolerate a stone of sin in your heart and you'll never be hundredfold fruitful. Furthermore, Jesus said you'll be dangerously vulnerable to stumbling in a time of trial or temptation (Mark 4:17). If you want to survive the heat of fiery troubles, remove your stones. Then your roots will be able to reach deeply into the moist subsoil of the word and Spirit, and you'll overcome.

Stones force our roots to stay close to the surface—at the shallow level of our feelings and emotions. Feelings and emotions are a gift from God, but by themselves won't sustain us in times of heat and pressure. To endure and overcome persecution, our roots must go deeper than our feelings and reach down into our convictions, values, and spirit—where we access the supply of the word of God and the Spirit. Stone removal, therefore, is essential.

A plant can survive a blazing sun and blistering temperatures if its roots go deep enough to access a constant supply of moisture. The same is true for us. When we remove our stones and send our roots deeply into the love of Christ, it doesn't matter what furnace blasts might assault us. The heat will make us even *more* fruitful.

This is personal for me. I know what it's like to be blindsided by a fiery trial. When I was thirty-five years old, I experienced a trial that shook me to the core and almost took me out. Stone removal became a matter of life and death. To survive the heat, I had to toss every stone I found and send my roots down deeper than ever into the words of Christ. When I did that, instead of the trial taking me out, it made me more fruitful than ever. My point is, I'm speaking from experience.

Zero toleration for stones has become my way of life. I have resolved that, by God's grace, whenever He shows me a stone that's hiding in my heart, I will deal immediately with it and get it out.

Zero toleration of stones will be even more important as we approach Christ's return, because trouble is only going to increase. Jesus said so: "In the world you will have tribulation" (John 16:33). There *is* an "evil day" (Eph 6:13)—that is, a day of unprecedented tribulation that will shake everything that can be shaken. Finances, career, marriage, family, friendships, health, faith—everything will be shaken. To survive, our roots must go deep.

Zero toleration for stones.

Greater heat, deeper reach.

The heat will reveal how you've handled your stones. It

will prove that you've removed your stones and that your roots are penetrating deeply into the love of Christ.

You're not simply going to survive, you're going to thrive!

Now let's look at some examples of stones.

CHAPTER 15

Surprised by Fear

We've said that stones are pockets of sin in our hearts that hinder root development. Let's get practical now, and look at some examples of stones. Let's start with the stone of fear.

Fear is a stone of compromise, and it can really surprise you in the way it suddenly shows up in your heart. When you're strong and secure, you might think to yourself, *Fear? Thanks be to God, I have no problem with fear. I know what God's word says about anxiety. He hasn't given me a spirit of fear, but of power, of love, and of a sound mind. My heart is fearless!*

And then along comes a seasonal disruption. Our world is shaken, and everything changes. In the swirl, it's possible to find ourselves suddenly looking at a stone of fear in our heart.

You may wonder, *Where did that stone come from? I can't even remember the last time I struggled with fear. Why has fear suddenly surfaced in my emotions?*

Answer: *change of seasons.*

As seasons change over a farmer's field, stones that were buried can work their way toward the surface and suddenly appear. The same can happen with our hearts. When our personal season changes, stones of compromise can surface in our hearts we didn't even know were there.

When I think about fear, I'm reminded of the COVID-19 pandemic that hit our world with fear in 2020. If you weren't old enough to remember 2020, let me explain what it was like. The pandemic suddenly burst upon the consciousness of the world in March of 2020. It was a *global* change of seasons. Businesses closed, people were hospitalized, several million died, churches were shuttered for months, students studied online, almost everybody wore masks, the whole world practiced social distancing, airports turned into ghost towns, political leaders were shaken by uncertainty and controversy, grocery stores were emptied, the supply of goods was interrupted, and the income stream of many was strangled. As though carried by the jet stream, a wave of disruption swept across the nations and gripped hearts everywhere with fear.

It was an international pandemic of fear, and in the maelstrom of the hysteria, many Christians suddenly found themselves looking at a stone of fear in their hearts they didn't even know was there. We were surprised by fear and anxiety.

Anxiety

Fear, worry, and anxiety are stones that hinder fruitfulness.

Let me qualify that by saying *anxiety attacks* might be in a slightly different category. Sometimes they seem to be more than just a stone—more like a stone with negative spiritual energy on it. For now, I'm not talking about the negative demonic energy that can sometimes attach to a stone. For now, I'm simply writing about old-fashioned, all-American, Adamic-nature anxiety. See anxiety as a stone in your garden.

Even though 2020 is well behind us, it seems we're still living in a global pandemic of anxiety. Millions are anxious about their health, finances, relationships, or jobs.

Let's be blunt. If you're anxious about something in your present circumstances, you've got yourself a stone.

Anxiety is illegal in the kingdom of God. Never make peace with your anxieties. Philippians 4:6 says, "Be anxious for nothing." *Nothing* means *nothing*. Anxiety is sin, and when we're anxious, it means we have a stone in our hearts that is hindering our fruitfulness.

Okay, full disclosure. I was tempted with anxiety during COVID-19. Let me explain.

My Struggle with Anxiety

When everyone suddenly realized, on March 15, 2020, that COVID was a global threat, the whole world shut down overnight. Thousands of airline flights were abruptly cancelled. Conferences worldwide were cancelled, and group gatherings—such as church services—were prohibited or strictly regulated.

This affected me in a personal way because, as an author and traveling speaker, I make my living from itinerant ministry and book sales. But many churches temporarily suspended all their weekly gatherings, and nobody knew how long the lockdown would last. In the uncertainty of it all, *every* ministry engagement in my calendar cancelled. Nobody knew from day to day what the future might hold. Pastors didn't know, from week to week, whether they could open their church doors or what new regulations the government might impose.

When my schedule erased, my income stream tanked. And as my income deflated, something else began to inflate in my heart: anxiety.

I was really surprised by this stone. I couldn't remember the last time I struggled with anxiety. I wondered, *Why am I suddenly feeling anxious?* The answer, of course, was *change of seasons.* COVID had brought a crazy, unforeseen season to the world, and it surfaced a stone in my heart that I didn't know was there. The global upheaval was enough of a season changer to bring my stone of anxiety to the surface.

Once I identified that stone, I went after it. It had to go! I found some of my favorite Scriptures related to anxiety, and I clung to them in prayer. My strongest verse was, "Be anxious for nothing" (Phil 4:6), with emphasis on the word *nothing.*

As I prayed and quoted God's word regarding anxiety, I made some headway in my soul, but a full release was slow in coming. If you're up for the story, I'll tell you what evicted that stone from my heart on that occasion.

My son Michael swung by our place on an errand, and I said to him, "Michael, you're going to be my confessor. I'm going to confess my sin to you, and in the spirit of James 5:16, you're going to pray for me so that I can be healed." As a reminder, James 5:16 says, "Confess your trespasses to one another, and pray for one another, that you may be healed."

I told Michael that I was being tempted with anxiety. I gave him the whole story, explained how I was being tempted, and repented in his presence. Then he prayed for me. His prayer was short and simple—I think less than a minute in duration—but that stone of anxiety was *immediately* uprooted and gone! To be honest, I was a bit surprised at the suddenness of my victory. Simply by obeying James 5:16, I was healed of the stone of anxiety and instantly experienced a release of joy in the Holy Spirit.

I discovered just how eager the Lord is to help us with stone removal.

James 5:16 is not necessarily the key to overcoming *every* struggle with anxiety. The Lord has different keys for different situations, but it was the key for me on that occasion.

No Worries

Anxiety engages in a battle for which there is no grace. Let me explain.

Jesus said, "Therefore do not worry about tomorrow, for tomorrow will worry about its own things. Sufficient for the day is its own trouble" (Matt 6:34). Worry and anxiety are always concerned about tomorrow and rarely about today. When we look at today, things seem okay because we have clothes to wear, food to eat, and a place to sleep. But when we look at tomorrow (the future) and imagine a threat to our future security, we can be tempted to become anxious.

But Jesus made it clear in Matthew 6:34 that we're to engage only with today's troubles. Furthermore, He taught us to pray only for today's daily bread, not tomorrow's (Matt 6:11). When we pray regarding today's troubles, He releases grace and lifts us to overcoming faith. But when we engage with tomorrow's troubles—that is, the difficulties that might possibly surface tomorrow—the Lord offers no help. He doesn't help us process tomorrow's troubles because we don't know what tomorrow will hold.

There's tremendous freedom in following Jesus' advice and refusing anxiety. When we become anxious about tomorrow, realize it's sin, repent, and resolve to engage with tomorrow's troubles tomorrow, His peace floods our hearts and we're assured of His care *right now*. Jesus wants us to live in this freedom and joy every day.

At the cross, Jesus showed us how to engage with life's troubles. He knew, long before the cross happened, about the horrors that awaited Him. And yet, as it drew closer, He refused to agonize in prayer over Calvary's troubles. Instead, He waited until the day of His arrest and crucifixion to pray for grace. When that day finally came, He entered Gethsemane and gave Himself fully to prayer over His impending sufferings. Because He waited to the day of His sufferings to agonize in prayer, He received strength from the Father to step forward and face His crucifixion with holy resolve.

Follow that example, and refuse to worry about tomorrow's troubles. Why exhaust yourself by fighting a battle that heaven isn't helping you with? Instead, concern yourself only with today's troubles. When you see something troubling about today, go to the throne and receive grace and mercy to help in your time of need (Heb 4:16).

Refuse anxiety. And if it should ever appear, dig it up and remove it from your heart.

Family Health History

I'll share another personal story about the stone of fear.

I was with my friends Chris and Joan Wood, and during our visit Joan reminded me that her mother had suffered a premature death from a heart attack. Consequently, Joan had feared that she might have inherited a congenital vulnerability to heart attacks. The fear of a heart attack and premature death had quietly nagged her for years.

She decided to go after that stone of fear, so she asked some friends to pray with her. As they prayed together, the fear lifted. Later, when she went to her doctor for a routine physical checkup, the doctor exclaimed that her EKG was *perfect*! Not only was the stone of fear removed from her heart, but Joan believed that the Lord had rejuvenated and renewed her body at the same time.

Later, as I reflected on her story, I asked myself, *I wonder if I have any fears or apprehensions related to the health history of my parents and family.* At first I thought the answer was *no*, but as I pondered it, I was surprised that the answer became *yes*. The apprehension was so small that I hadn't identified it until that moment. Upon close examination, I realized I had a small apprehension that I might lose my strength of mind in my final years like my father did. He suffered from dementia in his final years. I've inherited many of his qualities, and now I realized I had a quiet fear of also experiencing dementia in my sunset years.

It didn't feel like a huge boulder. It felt more like a pebble, but still, I clearly had a stone of fear in my heart. I decided to get out my shovel and go after it. I returned to Chris and Joan, and explained that I had identified a similar apprehension in my heart related to the health history of my family. I confessed my sin and asked them to pray for me. They prayed for me in a beautiful way, and I sensed that the pebble of fear was removed from the garden of my heart. Immediately, I rejoiced in 2 Timothy 1:7, "For God has not given us a spirit of fear, but of power and of love and of a sound mind."

How about you? Do you have any apprehensions in your soul related to the health history of your family? If the Lord shows you a stone of fear in your heart, ask Him to show you how to dig it up and remove it. Only a fearless heart can be hundredfold fruitful.

When removing a stone of compromise from your heart, replace it with its corresponding virtue. Replace fear with faith, fornication with chastity, addictions with self-control, anger with meekness, sloth with diligence, gluttony with temperance.

I hope these examples give you a practical grip on the kinds of stones that can hinder our pursuit of hundredfold fruitfulness. And there are even more examples to mention. In the next chapter, we'll look at a few more examples of stones.

CHAPTER 16

More Examples of Stones

The last chapter focused on the stone of fear, but there are many other stones that can also diminish our fruitfulness. To help us understand this terrain, let's look at some other examples of stones that can hinder our root development.

Some Stones That Hinder Roots

Unforgiveness. When we don't forgive, we're in clear disobedience to Jesus (Matt 6:12-15; 18:35). Therefore, we could call unforgiveness a stone. It's impossible to nurse a stone of unforgiveness in the heart and be hundredfold fruitful. If you identify a stone of unforgiveness in your heart, decide that it has to go. Forgive and keep on forgiving until that stone is entirely removed from your heart.

Anger. We're commanded in Scripture to refuse anger or to allow wrath a place in our hearts (James 1:19-20). If you struggle with anger or rage, it means there's a stone in your heart. Get out your shovel and go after the thing. Even if you don't know right now how to overcome the anger that suddenly wells up from within, resolve in your heart to never stop with your spade until the thing is completely removed from the garden of your heart.

Hatred. Hatred is a horrible stone, and it can completely kill the harvest of your heart (see 1 John 2:11). If you identify any hatred in your heart, go after it in Jesus' name! Repent, dig it up, and ask Jesus to replace it with His love. May your hatred for that person be replaced with such a pure love of Christ that you would lay your life down for them.

Cynicism. Many today are cynical about the church and Christianity. Cynicism views the intentions and integrity of people through a skeptical bent. It's easy for us to become cynical when we see flaws in church systems, or are hurt by people in our group, or see good things taken to excess. Somebody once called cynicism *frozen rage* because it can appear cool on the surface but underneath is a frigid weight of emotions. Cynicism thinks it holds the higher moral ground, and despises those it perceives as serving the irrelevant. Cynicism is fueled by pessimism, unbelief, and a scoffing spirit (see 2 Pet 3:3). God is cynical toward cynics (Prov 3:34). When cynicism starts to form inside, it shrivels the heart. I've never known a fruitful cynic. In the same way that Abraham threw a scoffing spirit out of his house, throw the stone of cynicism away from your heart (Gen 21:8-10). Replace it with the word of Jesus, "Only believe" (Mark 5:36).

Addictions. Addictions are sinful because they control our behavior, and we're not to be mastered by sin (John 8:34). Rather, we're called to be self-controlled and Spirit-led (Gal 5:23; Rom 8:14). If there's a compulsive behavior in your life, that stone is hindering your fruitfulness, maybe even more than you realize. Resolve with holy purpose that you're not going to nurse that indulgence, but you're going to resist it until you have victory. Grab your shovel, dig deep, stay with it until it's completely removed from your life, and then keep pressing forward for hundredfold fruitfulness.

Dating an unbeliever. We're told to marry only a believer in Christ (see 1 Cor 7:39; 2 Cor 6:14). Refuse to date unbelievers. If an unbeliever has romantic interest in you, refuse to let the friendship deepen until they're genuinely born again. If you're considering marrying someone who is an unbeliever, you're harboring a stone of compromise in your heart. Repent and get rid of that stone, or you'll never be hundredfold fruitful.

Foolish talking. Paul said that foolish talking or coarse jesting should not occur among saints (Eph 5:3-4). If your tongue is given to foolish banter, there's a stone in your heart. Don't ignore it—it's hindering your root system. Go after it and get that stone out of your garden.

Sexual sin. The general word that Scripture uses for sexual sin is fornication. *Fornication* includes virtually every kind of sexual sin, whether sex before marriage, rape, homosexuality, incest, adultery, etc. Jesus spoke very clearly against fornication (Matt 15:19). If you're practicing any kind of fornication, there's a clear and present danger in the garden of your heart. You're harboring a stone of compromise, and it's really undermining your fruitfulness. Repent, get rid of that stone, and reach for greater fruitfulness!

Lying. We're commanded by God to not steal or lie to one another (Lev 19:11). Lying is a stone that can completely destroy the fruitfulness of your heart (see Rev 21:8). If you're a liar, I charge you in the name of Jesus to repent and get rid of that stone!

Rebellion. Rebellion is a sin against God (1 Sam 15:23). If you sense a rebellious rock in your soul, go after it until it's removed from your heart. Replace rebellion with submission to God (James 4:7).

Racism. Racism is a stone that will hinder your fruitfulness. Racism places confidence in the flesh (see Phil 3:3)—that is, it views our flesh as superior to someone else's flesh because of skin color, or ethnicity, or accent, or upbringing. Renounce all racial prejudice and, instead, view others better than yourself (Phil 2:3). Any time you see the tiniest pebble of racism in your heart, get out your shovel.

Porn

Porn is a stone. If you struggle with compromise related to pornography, you've got a stone in your heart. Tolerate a stone of porn and you'll never be hundredfold fruitful. Instead, decide with holy resolve that you're going to turn your heart into an excavation site, go to work, and dig until that stone is entirely evicted from your garden.

I'm going to share a little bit of my own story here. I struggled every now and then with an occasional temptation to check out the TV channels to see if there might be a show with some skin. In my case, porn didn't seem like a huge boulder—maybe more like a pebble—but I knew it was limiting my fruitfulness.

One day in 2006, the Lord took me to Job 31:1, "I have made a covenant with my eyes; why then should I look upon a young woman?" The Lord invited me to make a covenant with my eyes, as Job had. The idea absolutely terrified me, but as I prayed I realized God was extending an invitation of grace. He seemed to be saying something like, "If you decide to make a covenant with your eyes, I will help you."

I decided to accept His gracious offer. I wrote down my eye covenant in my journal, dated it, and sealed it with a big offering. It was violent, but some battles require violence (Matt 11:12). I am so grateful to God now because, since that day, I have enjoyed victory over porn. The stone is gone. An eye covenant has been one of the most life-changing, helpful things I've ever done in the grace of God.

After living in the victory of an eye covenant for several years, the Lord directed me to write a book on it, titled *A Covenant With My Eyes*. It's available everywhere in paperback and all digital formats. It's also available in Spanish, Portuguese, Russian, Korean, Romanian, Arabic, and Chinese. If your experience with an eye covenant is as blessed as mine, it will get that stone out of the garden of your heart, and you will be more fruitful.

Don't See Any Stones?

If you're not aware of any stones of sin or compromise

in your heart, then enjoy your confidence in God. When the time is right, God will show you the next stone He wants you to target. In the meantime, enjoy Jesus!

The Christian life is not nonstop introspection. We're not called to a constant search for more stones. God's grace has removed condemnation from our lives (Rom 8:1). We've been liberated by Jesus into the delightful freedom of Spirit-filled living (Gal 5:1). Enjoy your freedom in the Spirit, and don't concern yourself with your stones—until He shows you another. In the meantime, bask in the joy of Christ and be filled with the Holy Spirit!

But when He shows you a stone of sin in your heart, then it's time to stop and do business with God. Get out your shovel, ask for grace, and go to work. The Holy Spirit is with you to help and empower you, but you alone can wield your shovel. Don't stop digging until the stone is completely removed from your heart.

Judas and Peter: A Study in Contrasts

When you see a stone, that means God is giving you grace to deal with it. He's showing it to you so He can help you remove it. But this truth comes with a warning. When God is giving you grace to overcome an area of compromise in your heart, it's dangerous to ignore it. That's why Paul wrote, "We…plead with you not to receive the grace of God in vain" (2 Cor 6:1). If you continue to tolerate a stone that God's grace is empowering you to overcome, that stone can severely hinder your fruitfulness and, in some tragic cases, even sideline you.

This truth is illustrated grimly in the life of Judas Iscariot. Judas was one of Jesus' twelve disciples, but he forfeited his spiritual inheritance because he refused to deal with his stones. Let me remind you about his story.

Judas struggled in his heart with carnal desires for

prominence, money, and influence. He acted on those desires by stealing from Jesus' money box (John 12:6).

Stealing is a stone. I call it a stone because we're told, "You shall not steal" (Exod 20:15). If we blatantly disobey one of the Lord's commands, we've got a stone—a pocket of sin—in our hearts. In the case of Judas, he had a stone of stealing in his heart.

Judas' stone was so huge that it wasn't simply hindering his fruitfulness, it was literally killing the garden of his heart. During the three years Jesus ministered with His disciples, He gave Judas many gentle opportunities to confess his stones, face them in the light, and deal with them. But Judas refused. He chose, again and again, to hide his stones.

The difficulty here is that persistent, unrepentant sin gives the god of this age permission to master us (see 2 Cor 4:4). When Judas denied God's grace and refused to dig up his stones, he granted Satan access to his soul. The same can happen with us. If we refuse to deal with stones in our hearts that God is showing us, we can eventually become susceptible to demonic energy in those areas.

In the end, Satan was able to enter Judas uninvited (Luke 22:3), use him like a puppet to betray Jesus, and then discard his soul to destruction. Judas' fate is dreadful both for what he forfeited and suffered. He forfeited a glorious inheritance as an apostle of the Lamb, and he suffered eternal condemnation. Jesus said of him, "It would have been good for that man if he had not been born" (Matt 26:24). More terrifying words were never spoken.

Peter was also one of Jesus' twelve disciples, and he also failed Jesus miserably, but yet his story ended dramatically differently. The reason is revealing. Here's a reminder about it.

Peter failed Jesus in lots of ways, but the most dramatic seems to have been when he denied Jesus three times during Jesus' trial (Matt 26:34). Like Judas, Peter had a lot of stones in his heart. But unlike Judas, Peter was an open book. Rather than hiding his issues, he brought them into the light and wrestled with them openly.

Peter was transparent about his stones, and consequently, Satan had to *ask permission* from God in order to sift Peter (Luke 22:31). In contrast, Judas was secretive about his stones, and consequently, Satan could enter Judas uninvited and drag him to destruction (Luke 22:3).

Peter had many issues but no secrets; Judas had many issues and many secrets.

Secrets. There it is, Judas had secrets. He hid his compulsive stealing from Jesus. He may have thought, *Jesus doesn't even know I'm stealing because, if He knew, He wouldn't give me the money box. Everybody thinks He knows so much, but He doesn't even know His own treasurer is stealing from the box!*

But Jesus saw Judas' secrets. Jesus sees our secrets, too. He invites us to bring our secret stones into the light so He can help us dig them up.

What do we learn from Judas and Peter? Never hide your stones from Jesus. Harbor no secrets. Even if you feel trapped by sin and don't know how to get it out of your garden, shine the light of honest transparency on it. Acknowledge it. Show the stone to Jesus. Repent. Repent by showing the stone to another mature disciple who can pray with you, strengthen you with Scripture, and hold you accountable spiritually.

Peter was transparent and honest about his stones and became the rock on which Jesus built His church (Matt 16:18). Deal openly with your stones and He'll make *you* a rock, too. You'll be a fortress of fruitfulness and a rock of stability in the body of Christ.

It bears repeating: Never hide your stones of compromise from Jesus.

- - - - - -

This concludes Part Three on the stones. Now let's talk about the weeds.

PART FOUR

THE WEEDS

CHAPTER 17

The Weeds

FOUR SOILS	HINDRANCE	MAIN ISSUE	CROP	TOOL
Trampled Heart	Birds	Unbelief	Stolen	Hoe
Shallow Heart	Stones	Tolerated Sin	Scorched	Shovel
Neglected Heart	Weeds	Distractions	Choked	Sickle
Fruitful Heart	All three	30/60/100-Fold	Productive	All three

Welcome to Part Four! We've looked at the birds and the stones, and now it's time to look at the weeds (or thorns) in the parable. Let's examine what they represent, how they can diminish our fruitfulness, and how we overcome.

I want to say five things about weeds.

Five Observations about Weeds

Firstly, every garden gets them. All you have to do to grow weeds is simply open a yard or garden. No need to plant them, weeds will just happen. They'll appear automatically, guaranteed. Nobody plants them, but every gardener gets them. Why? Because of the wind. Let me explain.

Weeds are seed factories. They produce zero fruit but countless seeds. When weeds release their seeds, the wind blows those seeds *everywhere*. Usually, they're too small to be noticed by the human eye, but you know seeds are there when you see birds pecking at the ground. Birds peck at the ground to gobble up the seeds that the wind has strewn across the countryside.

The wind blows the seeds of weeds onto every yard and garden. In a similar way, the winds of life blow the seeds of spiritual weeds onto the hearts of every Christian. No one is exempt—all Christians have weeds.

Secondly, weeds dominate. They grow faster than the good stuff, higher than the good stuff, wider than the good stuff, and thicker than the good stuff.

Weeds are bullies. They overshadow fruitful plants and commandeer most of the light, moisture, and nutrients that fruitful plants need. Jesus used the perfect word to describe this—weeds *choke*. They choke the health of good plants so they don't produce to full capacity.

Thirdly, weeds take a lot of hard work to suppress. For gardeners, weeding the garden is arguably the most tedious and annoying task of the year. And yet, to have a crop, they know weeding is essential.

Gardeners also know that the tedious task of weed control is made easier when the soil is wet. They'll go after the weeds early on, when the ground is damp and the roots young.

They're Back!

Fourthly, weeds come back. That's what I hate most about weeds. No matter how thoroughly I weed my garden, it's never enough. Weeds always come back.

I have lived on both the east and west coasts of America, and I thought I knew what weeds were. But no, I didn't know what weeds were until we moved to Missouri, the heartland of America. We now live on a wooded lot in Kansas City, and the weeds here have an attitude. They're ADHD. If you want to have a lawn or garden in Missouri, keeping your weeds at bay is just about a full-time job.

The underbrush around my house is hyperactive. It grows like crazy and is always encroaching on my lawn, landscaping, and garden. I've declared war, therefore, on my weeds. I don't know if people can tell by looking at me, but I'm a man at war. And I have an arsenal of artillery to help me in this war. For example, I have a powerful lawnmower, an edger, two chainsaws, hand shears, pruning shears, and clippers.

When I have my weapons in hand, the weeds shudder with dread. Weed clippings fly in every direction. I attack them like a man on a mission.

There comes a moment, sometime in the fall, when I finally seem to gain the victory. It comes with a sigh of relief. *Finally! I've won!* The weeds and underbrush have been pummeled into submission.

But then the following spring? *They're back!* And with a vengeance. They're bigger, bolder, and angrier than ever. What can be done? My only recourse is to return to my arsenal, get out the artillery, and resume the war. Because when it comes to weeds, the war is never over.

One of the general differences between stones and weeds: Once you remove a stone from your garden, it's gone; but when you remove a weed from your garden, it's never gone. It's just replaced with ten more weeds of the same nasty variety.

In our parable, therefore, weeds represent areas of struggle in our hearts that seem to resurface over and over.

When it comes to weeds, you'll never eradicate them from your life. You might enjoy a temporary respite, but then they reappear again. Applied to our lives spiritually, there are some issues we never fully overcome but fight against them all our lives until our race is over.

When I understood this, it didn't discourage me—as though I were fighting an unwinnable war. Rather, it encouraged me, and here's why. In the past, when a weed would resurface in my heart, I would struggle with accusation. The accuser would whisper, "You never dealt with that issue in real sincerity. If you had been sincere with God, it wouldn't be surfacing again. But you're a hypocrite and a half-hearted repenter. Your repentance wasn't real, and your obedience wasn't real. Stop pretending that you're a sincere disciple of Jesus."

But now I realize that, when weeds resurface in my heart, this is normative for disciples of Jesus. This understanding has silenced the enemy's accusations. I'm struggling with weeds again, not because I'm insincere, but because weeds always come back.

The only thing we can do with weeds is keep pulling them and cutting them back. Prepare yourself, therefore, to take a sickle to your weeds for the rest of your life. Because just about the time you think you've gotten victory over your weeds, *they're back.*

Weeds Can Have a Positive Role

And fifthly, weeds actually have a helpful purpose—in the right context. My friend Andy Jennings, who is an agriculturalist, put me onto this. He told me that weeds fulfill a positive purpose on uncultivated land. How? By protecting fallow ground from wind and water erosion. Additionally, the roots of weeds help work the soil. Later, when weeds die, they fertilize the soil.

On fallow ground, weeds can be friends; on cultivated ground, weeds are enemies.

One example of this is seen on golf courses. Groundskeepers intentionally allow weeds to grow in the rough—that is, the peripheral areas around a fairway where you're not supposed to hit your ball. If they see you hit your golf ball into the thick weeds of the rough, they'll smile as they watch you flail and thrash to rescue your ball from the weeds. They'll think, *Good luck with that one. Serves you right for hitting your ball into the rough.*

But on a green? Or on a fairway? If a weed is so bold as to make an appearance on a green, that weed will suffer the wrath and weaponry of the groundskeeper. He'll be on that weed like white on rice. Groundskeepers have zero tolerance for weeds on the fairways or greens of golf courses.

I handle weeds on my property the same way. If a weed appears in my lawn or garden, I'll attack it. But there are places on the periphery of my property where I actually *want* weeds to grow in a controlled way. Why? Because they protect the soil, during times of torrential rain, from undesirable erosion.

Applied to our lives, weeds represent things that we don't necessarily want to eradicate completely from our lives, but we want them properly controlled in the periphery of our hearts. More on that in a bit.

What Are the Weeds?

What do the weeds in Jesus' parable represent? Thankfully, He Himself told us: "The cares of this world, the deceitfulness of riches, and the desires for other things" (Mark 4:19). Luke, in his rendering, is even more concise: "cares, riches, and pleasures of life" (Luke 8:14).

The weeds are cares and pleasures. Cares relate to the difficult side of life; pleasures relate to the enjoyable side of life. And both are empowered by money. Cares and pleasures—and money. Those are the weeds.

Weeds are temporary elements that make life in this passing world workable and enjoyable. Cares involve the task of making life *workable*; pleasures regard the things in life that are *enjoyable*. Both are *temporary*. The temporary wants to choke the eternal; the fruitless wants to choke the fruitful.

Cares and *pleasures* describe opposite influences—things *unpleasant* and *pleasant*. Cares are unpleasant concerns that deplete and exhaust us, such as the fight to stay afloat financially. Pleasures are delights that exhilarate and entertain us, such as vacations and good food.

In other words, some weeds are bitter, and some are sweet—and all are bankrolled by deceitful riches.

The tools in Chart 1—hoe, shovel, and sickle—are images that can represent how we respond to our weeds. If you have hardness in your heart, use something like a *hoe* to break up your fallow ground. If you have a stone of compromise in your heart, use something like a *shovel* to dig and remove it. If you have weeds in your heart, use something like a *sickle* to hack them back.

I'm using a sickle to represent how we control our weeds. But in the natural, weeds are actually treated in several ways. Some weeds are zapped with a preemergent, while others are sprayed. Some weeds are pulled, while others are cut back. As we look at various kinds of weeds in the next chapters, the Lord will give you specific strategies to go after each weed that tries to choke your heart.

Let's look at the weeds, "The cares of this world, the deceitfulness of riches, and the desires for other things" (Mark 4:19), and examine what Jesus meant by these three designations.

CHAPTER 18

Deceitfulness of Riches

Jesus identified three kinds of weeds in His parable: "The cares of this world, the deceitfulness of riches, and the desires for other things entering in choke the word, and it becomes unfruitful" (Mark 4:19). Putting the three together, *weeds are temporary elements that make life in this passing world workable and enjoyable.*

Let's start with the first kind of weed He mentioned, the *cares of this world.*

The Cares of This World

The cares of everyday life are unpleasant weeds that every household grapples with. These weeds regard the daily challenge to make life in this world *workable.* Bills, groceries, clothes for the kids, schedules, errands, education costs, business challenges, career, rent, loans, vehicles, health insurance, retirement preparations—we have so many cares that need attention. As we manage them, it's tempting to become so engrossed in them that we neglect the fruitful.

The original Greek word for *cares* means *to divide the mind.* It describes someone who is torn between two foci. In this case, we're torn between the temporary and the eternal. As earth dwellers, we have one eye on our temporary needs; as citizens of heaven, we have the other eye on things with eternal value. Just as weeds choke the vitality of a fruit bearing plant, the emporary can choke the eternal in our lives.

In my quest for greater fruitfulness, it helps me to think temporary versus eternal. Because of this parable, I frequently ask myself questions such as, *Am I doing something right now that is temporary or eternal? Will this activity produce eternal fruit, or will it maintain things that are for this life only?* Just asking myself those questions helps keep my priorities clear.

For example, I own a book publishing business that I operate out of my home. To grow a business requires a lot of time and hard work. I've discovered that the demands to make a business profitable can overgrow our hearts like weeds. There comes a point when a business owner or career professional may say to themselves, *I've worked my job enough for today. Before the day is over, I'm going to do something that is eternally fruitful.*

Now, as mentioned in Chapter Eight, there's a measure in which our diligence to earn income can be fruitful, in the sense that our income provides security for our family, it enables us to finance kingdom endeavors, and it gives us financial stability so we can devote our discretionary time to fruitful pursuits. But the very career that can enable us to be fruitful, if not managed carefully, can overtake our hearts like a weed and choke the very fruitfulness we desired.

What should we do when we feel like our heart is being overrun by the cares of this life? Get out your sickle! *Swing that thing!* Be violent about it, and get the cares of life back in the periphery of your heart where they belong. Renew your resolve to seek first the kingdom of God and His righteousness (Matt 6:33).

Now let's look at the second variety of weed that Jesus mentioned, the *deceitfulness of riches.*

The Deceitfulness of Riches

Jesus said it bluntly: *Money is deceitful.* It lies to us. It doesn't deliver on its promises. It doesn't deliver the things it promised (such as happiness, fulfillment, and security), and then it delivers the things it promised it wouldn't (such as grief, sorrow, and heartache). Money never tells the whole truth.

Jesus was saying money talks. It's always speaking lies—with a powerfully believable voice. All the nations are deceived by money's voice. Your family, coworkers, and friends are deceived by its voice. And your heart is also easily wooed by its crooning voice.

Have you heard any of money's lies? Here's a few of them:

You need more of me. Stop and examine that claim, and you'll realize it's not true. The true need in our lives is not for more money, but for more of the light of the knowledge of Christ. Money says that I need Jesus plus money, but I'm declaring that *He is all I need* (Col 2:2-3). Jesus plus nothing. What I *really* need is more of the faith and love that reside in the heart of Christ (1 Tim 1:14).

Without me you can do nothing. Hmm, I thought I heard Someone else say that once.

With me you'll be happy. But it's a lie. There are countless stories of people who experienced a financial windfall, only to end in miserable ruin. Were they initially happy when they first received the bonanza? Yes. But the joy proved to be hollow, and their story ended in broken emptiness. Money simply can't give us the happiness, joy, and contentment that is available to us in Christ.

Here's another of money's lies: *Get more of me, and you'll get more power, influence, and significance.* In one sense, it's true that money might give you more power and influence with acquaintances, but its power is on a playing field that lacks eternal significance. Money doesn't give you more power or influence with God. In fact, if you try to use money to gain influence with God, you'll come under the curse of Simon: "But Peter said to Simon, 'Your money perish with you, because you thought that the gift of God could be purchased with money!'" (Acts 8:20). Many millionaires are full on money but empty on significance. If we get our identity from money, it will evaporate at our passing, and we'll die a nothing.

Always remember that I supply your needs. Not true!

God's word assures that our needs are met, not by money, but by Him: "God shall supply all your need according to His riches in glory by Christ Jesus" (Phil 4:19). Money is never the believer's source.

Only the rich have a problem with avarice. That's another big lie. Greed tempts people of every economic strata.

You can't do the will of God without me. What a colossal lie! This one has deceived many of God's servants. Some people in the church have been persuaded that they need money to bring the kingdom of God to their city and region. Yes, money can help fund ministry initiatives, but we don't actually need it to do God's will. Want an example? Remember Peter's famous words to the cripple, "Silver and gold I do not have, but what I do have I give you: In the name of Jesus Christ of Nazareth, rise up and walk" (Acts 3:6). Peter didn't need money to bring the kingdom of God to that cripple and release him from his hell hole. Neither do we.

You don't have a problem with money. Money really wants you to believe this one. The weed of money wants you to believe it has no choke hold on your heart. Why? Because then you'll leave the weed alone. When it comes to money, never trust your heart.

Jeremiah wrote, "The heart is deceitful above all things, and desperately wicked; who can know it?" (Jer 17:9). Money is deceitful, and so is our heart. Our heart wants to think that it has risen above the love of money. But Jeremiah said we don't even know the deceitful things that are lurking inside our own heart. Therefore, it's worth repeating: *When it comes to money, never trust your heart.* Always keep in mind that your heart is susceptible to being choked by money's sinister foliage.

Money Is a Weed

Not all Bible teachers seem to agree with Jesus on this point, but Jesus was quite clear in the parable: Money is a weed.

Why would Jesus depict money as a weed? Because it's not eternal. There is no money in heaven. Its value is for this life only. As such, it's a fruitless weed that's always trying to overgrow our hearts.

Let me qualify my meaning. As stated in Chapter Seven, we can use filthy money, through wise stewardship, to store up treasure in heaven. And again, just as weeds have a helpful role in a secondary way to minimize erosion of uncultivated soil, money is somewhat helpful in our lives when kept in the periphery. Said succinctly, *money has a useful role in our lives when it's kept in a peripheral place in our hearts.*

We're not trying to eradicate money from our lives. Rather, we're laboring to keep it out of the garden of our affections. We still handle money, but very carefully. We're not going to stop growing our career, paying the bills, and feeding the kids. But in the process, we're going to swing our sickle and keep cutting back money's attempts to make camp in the center of our hearts.

The problem is, money doesn't want to stay peripheral. Weeds never do. Using our earlier golf analogy, money doesn't want to stay in the rough of our lives; it wants to get on the fairway and the green of our hearts. It wants *everywhere.* Like a weed, it's constantly extending its reach to encroach our heart.

What are we going to do about that? We're going to keep reaching for our sickle! We're going to keep whacking back the love of money that wants to choke our hearts.

How do we swing our sickle? Through generosity. Every time you give generously in the name of Christ, you're pushing money back into the periphery of your heart.

People Who Got Choked

The Bible gives many examples of people whose hearts were choked by money. I'll mention a few here.

Balaam. Balaam saw visions of God and heard the audible voice of God, and yet got taken out by covetousness (Num 24:16). Just how sinister is this weed?

Gehazi. Gehazi was the servant of Elisha who succumbed to the love of money and, as a result, became a leper (2 Kings 5:27). His story warns us that covetousness is as deadly as leprosy.

The rich young man of Matthew 19:16-24. Jesus gave him the offer of a lifetime—to shadow Him in His traveling ministry. Who wouldn't jump at that? But the young man's heart was overgrown with avarice, and when Jesus called him to sell all, he went away sorrowful.

Judas Iscariot. Judas was one of Jesus' twelve disciples, but his heart was overgrown with covetousness. He negotiated a deal so he could make money off Jesus' crucifixion (Matt 26:15). What a horrifying possibility, that the same weed that delivered Jesus to His crucifiers also wants to choke my heart.

Money—Jesus called it "unrighteous mammon" (Luke 16:9). *Unrighteous* indicates there's something inherently sinister about it. Paul wrote about "the mystery of lawlessness," and the way money works on the human heart is truly mysterious (2 Thess 2:7). Money got Jesus crucified (Matt 26:15); therefore, when you handle it, let your hands tremble and your lips quiver.

Violent Giving

Okay, full disclosure. I have a problem with money. Specifically, I'm tempted sometimes with the love of money. Whenever I feel it wrapping around my heart again, I get out my sickle and do violence to those weeds. I remind myself that I can't serve both God and money (Matt 6:24). Money wants to master my heart, but by the grace of God, I shall master it. I'm resolved, with God's help, to resist the love of money. God is my Master, not money, and I will love and serve Him only. Therefore, when money wants to master my heart, I begin to swing my sickle.

How do I swing my sickle? By devoting myself in a renewed way to almsgiving and generosity. That's the way Jesus told us to do it (see Luke 11:41). When I'm giving offerings to the poor and to the work of the kingdom, I'm hacking back money's nasty tentacles. I swing my sickle until my eyes are free of money's entanglements and back again on the face of Christ. Then I rejoice in my restored victory. Ah, the joy of quelling money's mastery!

But come back a year later, and guess what. *It's ba-a-a-ack.* Like a weed, the tendrils of money have crept back and are again trying to master my heart. What do I do? I get my sickle out all over again. I do whatever it takes—even if it means violent giving—to get money back in the periphery and away from the affections of my heart.

I'm reminded of the beautiful words of this hundred-year-old hymn:

Turn your eyes upon Jesus
Look full in His wonderful face
And the things of earth will grow strangely dim
In the light of His glory and grace.[1]

The third kind of weed that Jesus mentioned was *desires for other things.* For that one, come to the next chapter.

---

1 Helen Howarth Lemmel, "Turn Your Eyes Upon Jesus," 1918.

CHAPTER 19

Desires for Other Things

We've looked at *the cares of this world* and *the deceitfulness of riches;* now, let's consider the third variety of weeds Jesus identified, *the desires for other things* (Mark 4:19).

With this designation, Jesus was pointing to our common desire to make our brief time on earth *enjoyable.* In Luke's chronicle of this parable, Jesus called this one "the pleasures of life" (Luke 8:14). The weeds are *desires* (Mark 4:19) and *pleasures* (Luke 8:14), and they try to choke our fruitfulness.

Look again at the three kinds of weeds Jesus mentioned. *The cares of this world* refers to the tough side of life, the *desires for other things* refers to the easy side of life, and between the two is the engine of money—*the deceitfulness of riches*—that drives it all.

Pleasures and Purchases

We're created for pleasure (see Ps 16:11; Eccl 2:24). We're made to incline naturally toward the enjoyable things of life such as entertainment, recreation, distractions, creature comforts, relaxation, hobbies, vacations, shopping, good food, good drink, and good company.

When a chunk of free time opens, our default is usually toward the *pleasures of life.* We want to grab some grub, meet up with friends, do something fun, get on a device, improve our living space, etc. But Jesus said our *desires for other things* are weeds that can choke the fruitfulness of our hearts.

When it comes to the pleasures of life, one of the first things I think of is my favorite football team. I enjoy watching the Kansas City Chiefs—my home team—on TV when they're playing football. I'm a big fan! But I have a fresh awareness now, because of this parable, that time in front of the TV is fruitless. Not that it's inherently bad or wrong. My conscience doesn't condemn me because I'm watching a football game. It's not an issue of sin but of fruitfulness. If I allow myself too much TV, it will choke and diminish my fruitfulness.

How do I swing my sickle on that weed? I minimize the amount of time I allow myself to watch TV. Part of me would actually enjoy watching more TV, but Jesus' parable has awakened my desire for greater fruitfulness. Therefore, I willingly limit my screen time.

TV football is just one example of many pleasures of life. Which pleasures are most appealing to you? Whatever they might be, Jesus' parable will motivate you to gladly limit how much time and money you give to those desires.

Do you like to go shopping? Some of us do, but the desire for new purchases is a weed that can choke our hearts. How? By taking the time and resources that could have been used for greater fruitfulness, and using them instead on new stuff.

Stuff. That's a good word for it.

Stuff

I like stuff. You like stuff. All of us like to get new stuff, but the desire for more stuff can choke the heart.

Stuff is temporary, fruit is eternal.

We call the desire for more stuff *materialism*. Jesus' term for it was *desires for other things*.

Materialism—the desire for more stuff—is a weed that tries to engulf our hearts. We might get victory over it, but then it grows back again. To stay free of its fingers, we have to swing our sickle, over and over.

I've decided that I'm not going to buy new stuff simply because I can afford it. One way I swing my sickle is by restraining myself from buying something I can afford. I'm going to be generous with others and frugal with myself. Why? Because I don't want desires for stuff to choke my fruitfulness.

How can we use our sickle to cut back the weeds of materialism? One way Jesus provided was both remarkable and violent: "Sell what you have and give alms" (Luke 12:33).

Ask yourself this question: *When was the last time I obeyed this word of Christ? When was the last time I sold a possession and gave the proceeds to the poor?*

It's a great way to cut back the weeds of materialism.

Can we find someone in the Bible whose life illustrated how *desires for other things* choked the fruitfulness of their heart? Yes, I think one of the clearest examples was Lot's wife.

Lot's Wife

The story of Lot's wife is truly tragic. In fact, Jesus highlighted her tragic ruin when He urged us, "Remember Lot's wife" (Luke 17:32). Let's recap her story.

Lot and his wife moved into Sodom because it was an attractive, prosperous city. Lot's wife loved her new home. She loved the food, drink, standard of living, merchandise, relaxed lifestyle, music, availability of services, and sophistication of cosmopolitan living (see Ezek 16:49-50). She loved her stuff. Sodom was a good fit.

God decided to destroy Sodom, however, because of its sin. In His mercy, He sent two angels to rescue Lot and his family from Sodom's destruction. The angels took them by the hand and literally pulled them out of the city. As they hurried, the angels commanded them not to look back, but to flee with their eyes straight ahead.

Lot's wife, however, turned and looked back at Sodom. She must have been sorrowful for everything she was losing. She was losing the daughters who were left behind, her house, her possessions, her lifetime savings, and her city.

It seems she was torn. (As a reminder, the Greek word in our text for *cares* means to *divide the mind.*) Part of her wanted to obey God and join her husband in following the angel; the other part wanted to stay in Sodom. She had a divided heart. The weeds of Sodom's pleasures had overrun her heart and affections.

How could she leave the city she loved? With one last wistful glance, she looked back at her heart's home—and became in that instant a pillar of salt (Gen 19:26). Her example says to me, "Don't make an earthly city your home."

Who was Lot? Lot was the righteous man in the Bible who lost his sense of journey. He made Sodom home, and positioned his family to be choked by *desires for other things.*

What have I learned from Lot and his wife? That I must jealously preserve my identity as a pilgrim. Heaven is my home (Phil 3:20). I have no home here. I'm a sojourner and pilgrim on earth. As God helps me, the weeds of desires and pleasures will not encircle my heart. I'm going to keep cutting them back, consigning them to the periphery of my life, and reserving the garden of my heart for Jesus only.

Before we close this chapter, are there any other weeds we could mention? Yes. We could speak of jealousies, selfish ambitions, dissensions, envy, the pride of life, the fear of man, etc. (see Gal 5:19-21; 1 John 2:16). I view those things as weeds. But lest this chapter grow too long, we're going to examine only one more: comparisons.

I consider the sin of comparisons a weed.

Comparisons

Comparison is a nasty weed that hinders fruitfulness because it makes our comrades competitors. It takes our eyes off Jesus and gets us looking at how others are running their race. And yet, nasty as it is, it's a universal temptation.

According to one study, we spend twelve percent of our daily thoughts comparing ourselves with others.[1] This one is huge.

Comparisons never made of anyone a more fruitful disciple. If we perceive ourselves *superior* to our neighbor in a certain way, we'll be tempted with *pride*. If we perceive ourselves *inferior* to our neighbor in a certain way, we'll be tempted with *envy, insecurity, rivalry,* or *discouragement*.

What does Scripture say about comparisons?

Paul addressed this weed when he wrote, "For we dare not class ourselves or compare ourselves with those who commend themselves. But they, measuring themselves by themselves, and comparing themselves among themselves, are not wise" (2 Cor 10:12). The evaluation of our lives will not be based on how we compare with others, but how we compare to Christ and His upward call on our lives.

When Peter was tempted to compare himself to John, Jesus said, "What is that to you? You follow Me" (John 21:22). The call of God on someone else's life is not our concern. We keep our eyes on Jesus and follow Him.

Comparisons often stir envy, and James said that where there's envy, "confusion and every evil thing are there" (James 3:16).[2] It's impossible to become more fruitful when *confusion and every evil thing* are at work in our hearts. Those weeds choke fruit!

Comparison is a weed. Why would I classify it as a weed? Because it always comes back. You can repent of it, stomp on it, and grind it into the ground, but the temptation to compare invariably returns.

The only thing you can do with the weed of comparisons is keep cutting it back. Keep repenting. Keep swinging your sickle. And realize you'll probably war with comparisons for the rest of

---

1 Brian Ford, at https://www.selfimprovementdailytips.com/podcast/12-percent-comparison#:~:text=Are%20you%20ready%20to%20hear,spent%20comparing%20yourself%20to%20others

2 See my book *ENVY: The Enemy Within.*

your life. We don't mature past it, we just learn to repent faster.

A Personal Comparison Story

On one occasion, I was preparing to speak at a certain conference and seemed to be working harder than usual at my preparation. I kept polishing, over and over, the message that I planned to deliver. I realized I was working harder than usual to prepare for this event, so I remarked to my wife, "I don't know why I'm so uptight about preparing for this conference."

Her response was immediate. She came right back at me, "It's because you're looking at the other conference speaker's strengths, and you compare your weakness to his strength." I was busted. She had nailed the issue: comparison. Comparison had me in a knot.

I have repented of the sin of comparison *many* times through the years, but after my wife identified that it was there again, I had to make an altar with God and repent all over again.

I got my sickle out.

Kneeling before the Lord, I prayed, "I'm asking You to give me something that will help me do warfare with this tendency in my soul toward comparison. Give me a verse, or give me a sound bite. Help me fight this weed."

In response, the Lord graciously gave me this sound bite: *Comparisons choke the heart.*

I took that sound bite with me to the conference, and every time I was tempted to compare myself with the other speaker's strengths, I grabbed hold of that sound bite. *Comparisons choke the heart.* Comparison wanted to choke my gratefulness for everything God had given me. I used that sound bite like a man swinging a sickle on nasty weeds. How did it go? I'm pleased to say that my soul was delightfully free of the weed of comparison at that conference. Furthermore, I'm going to continue to use that sound bite whenever I need it. I've got my sickle ready, and when the weed of comparison shows up again, I've got a sound bite from the Lord in my arsenal.

Pursue Hundredfold Fruitfulness!

Let me remind you how Jesus closed the parable. He described someone who hears the word with a good heart and produces fruit.

> **But these are the ones sown on good ground, those who hear the word, accept it, and bear fruit: some thirtyfold, some sixty, and some a hundred (Mark 4:20).**

If we're not yet hundredfold fruitful, it means we still have areas in our heart that are hardened, or we're harboring stones of compromise, or we've got weeds choking our heart. Or we've got all three! But we're not discouraged by this. Rather, we're incentivized by Jesus to overcome and keep edging closer to hundredfold fruitfulness.

Receive holy motivation from Jesus. Break up the hard patches! Remove the stones! Cut back the weeds! You don't have to wait for your season to change—now is the time to become more fruitful.

May you impact the lives of everyone you touch with the love of Christ. May people's esteem of the Father be elevated because of your influence. May you grow in fruitfulness.

Are you fortyfold fruitful? Jesus is giving you grace to reach for forty-onefold. Are you sixty-eightfold fruitful? Reach for sixty-ninefold.

God's word urges us, "Keep your heart with all diligence, for out of it spring the issues of life" (Prov 4:23). How do we keep our heart? By wisely working our hoe, shovel, and sickle.

Jesus is releasing grace to you! He's helping you break up

every fallow patch, remove every stone of compromise, and cut back every encroaching weed.

You're going to bear more fruit!

- - - - - -

We've now completed our examination of the birds, stones, and weeds. In Part Five, we're going to look at the parable from a different angle. We're going to examine what's going on at the thirtyfold and sixtyfold crisis points, because navigating those two transitions successfully is essential for increased fruitfulness. Get ready for the parable to really land now.

PART FIVE

30-60-100

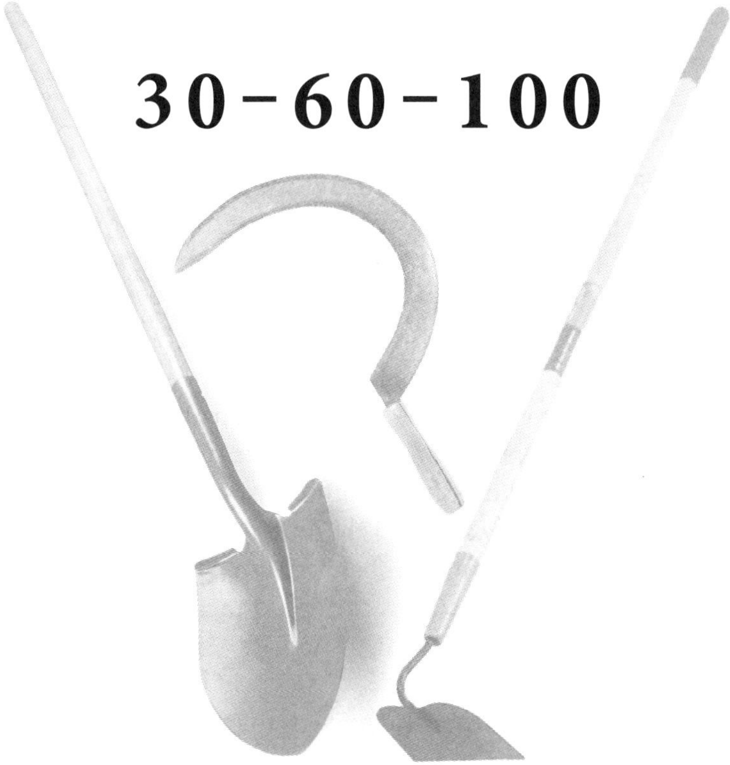

CHAPTER 20

Three Stages of Fruitfulness

Welcome to Part Five! We're now going to turn and look at our parable from a different vantage. We're going to explore the terms *thirtyfold, sixty, and a hundred*, as they describe our growth in fruitfulness.

> **But these are the ones sown on good ground, those who hear the word, accept it, and bear fruit: some thirtyfold, some sixty, and some a hundred (Mark 4:20).**

Jesus designated *thirtyfold, sixty, and a hundred* to indicate that believers bear fruit to God in differing degrees. Additionally, He was showing that He wants us to *grow* in fruitfulness, from thirty to a hundred.

None of us are stuck in a static slot or category of fruitfulness for our entire lives. In other words,

God doesn't call anyone to thirtyfold fruitfulness and no more. Rather, we're all on a growth curve, and we're all invited to reach for hundredfold fruitfulness.

Our calling and capacity is hundredfold fruitfulness, and our current attainment is probably only a percentage of hundredfold. Nobody goes from thirtyfold to sixtyfold fruitfulness. We go from thirty to thirty-one. It's a spectrum, and we grow incrementally.

Jesus gave the parable to *invite* us to grow, but more than that, to *motivate* us to grow. The wisdom of the parable incentivizes us to reach for greater fruitfulness. The fact that we've attained only a percentage of hundredfold doesn't discourage us; rather, it encourages us because we realize today's attainment is not the end of the story. Jesus is leading us into more!

Mysteries

The designations of *thirty, sixty, and a hundred* raise a question. Since we're all on a growth curve, Jesus could have easily said something like, "The ones on good ground bear fruit, anywhere from onefold to hundredfold." But instead of speaking about one to a hundred, He used three numbers. Why? This is a *mystery*. What do we mean by *mystery*? Well, look at what Jesus meant when He used that word:

> **To you it has been given to know the mystery of the kingdom of God; but to those who are outside, all things come in parables (Mark 4:11).**

In Matthew 13:11, Jesus used the plural *mysteries*. There are mysteries in the kingdom. *Kingdom mysteries are spiritual truths that are not readily evident at first observation but can be mined and uncovered through diligent digging.* Mysteries are not truths that God meant to keep hidden from us; rather, they're spiritual nuggets He wants us to find. They're not found through casual reading, however. To mine them, you've got to launch a search. Like veins of gold in the ground, they're lodes that beckon. Understanding is available but can be missed.

Every parable of Jesus' was an invitation to explore the mysteries of the kingdom.

We're dealing with embedded mysteries, so let's not gloss over parables too hastily. I hear Jesus saying, "Not so fast. Don't move past this parable so quickly. There's more here than you're seeing right now."

Let's slow down, therefore, and consider some of the mysteries hidden in Jesus' designations of *thirty, sixty*, and a *hundred*. That's what Part Five of this book is about.

Stages and Crisis Points

Thirty, sixty, and *hundred* point to three stages of fruitfulness. Maybe there's a better word than *stages*, such as *levels*, or *categories*, or *realms* of fruitfulness. But for now, we'll use *stages*.

Jesus' three markers indicate that there are three stages of consecration and growth in a disciple's life. We cross from one stage to the next at two *crisis points*. Perhaps it would be better to call these *thresholds*, or *barriers*, or *crossings*, or *transitions*, or *hurdles*. But for now, let's use the term *crisis points*.

The mystery in the three stages is pointing to a three-stage pattern for how disciples progress in spiritual maturity. The life stories of several people in Scripture align into three such stages. Moses' life, for example, easily divides into three stages:

- From age 1 to 40
- From age 40 to 80
- From 80 to 120

In Moses' case, he matured successfully through all three stages of fruitfulness. God testified that Moses was faithful in all of His house (Num 12:7), meaning (in part) that Moses was faithful at each stage of fruitfulness and at the two crisis points of transition.

Chart 2 is meant to help us visualize these three stages of fruitfulness.

Chart 2

Three Stages of Fruitfulness

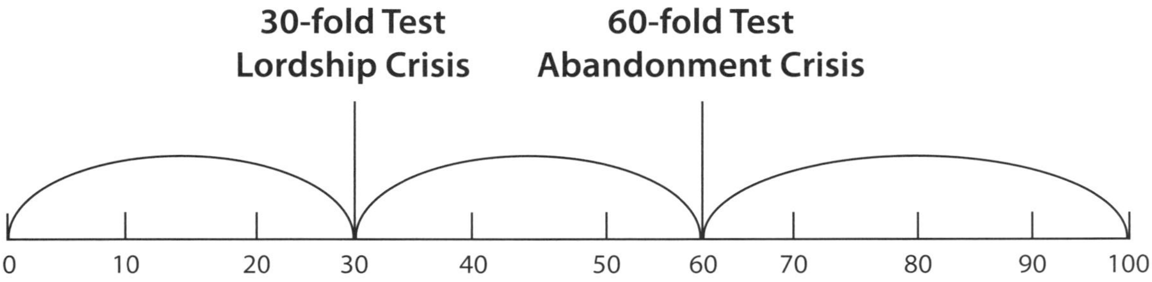

1 John 2:12-14	Children	Young Men	Fathers
Joseph	At Home	Potiphar's House	Palace
Moses	Pharaoh's House	Midian Wilderness	Israel's Leader
David	Shepherd	Captain	King
Jesus	Childhood	Earthly Ministry	Father's Right Hand

Three Stages

The clearest biblical witness to these three stages of fruitfulness, besides our parable, is found in John's writings:

> **I write to you, little children, because your sins are forgiven you for His name's sake. I write to you, fathers, because you have known Him who is from the beginning. I write to you, young men, because you have overcome the wicked one. I write to you, little children, because you have known the Father. I have written to you, fathers, because you have known Him who is from the beginning. I have written to you, young men, because you are strong, and the word of God abides in you, and you have overcome the wicked one. (1 John 2:12-14).**

John's terminology for the three stages of maturity was *little children, young men*, and *fathers*. By *little children*, he didn't mean toddlers of a young age, but rather *spiritual* children. Sometimes spiritual maturity has no connection to chronological age. Christians of all age groups can be *little children* spiritually. It's possible, for example, for someone to be elderly in chronological years but only a little child in terms of spiritual growth and fruitfulness.

How could that be? Well, maybe that elderly person became a believer in Christ just a few weeks ago, and they're still a babe in Christ. Or maybe that elderly person hit a crisis point and didn't progress past it. Therefore, *little children* refers to someone's spiritual not natural maturity.

Next, John addressed *young men*, but he didn't simply mean people in their twenties or thirties. He meant spiritual not chronological maturity. When it comes to fruitfulness, Christians of almost all age levels can potentially be termed *young men*.

Next, John addressed *fathers*. He wasn't thinking about gray-headed people, but rather the *spiritually* mature. In this instance, however, there seems to be a stronger connection between spiritual fathers and chronological age. For example, I've never met a teenager whom I considered to be a spiritual father. Most spiritual fathers I've met are also older in chronological years. Why? Because the processes that bring someone into spiritual fatherhood often take years or decades to develop.

Joseph is an exception here. He was a spiritual father to Pharaoh at age thirty-nine (see Gen 45:8). That's young! The reason Joseph attained spiritual fatherhood at such a young age was because of prison. God used the intensity of prison to accelerate Joseph's maturity. Prison is God's accelerated program. When Joseph ascended from prison at age thirty, he stepped into hundredfold fruitfulness as Egypt's prime minister.

We have more to say about *little children, young men*, and *fathers*. Come to the next chapter as we examine how John described these three stages of growth and fruitfulness.

CHAPTER 21

Little Children, Young Men, Fathers

I write to you, little children, because your sins are forgiven you for His name's sake. I write to you, fathers, because you have known Him who is from the beginning. I write to you, young men, because you have overcome the wicked one. I write to you, little children, because you have known the Father. I have written to you, fathers, because you have known Him who is from the beginning. I have written to you, young men, because you are strong, and the word of God abides in you, and you have overcome the wicked one. (1 John 2:12-14).

Little Children

When John addressed *little children*, he was writing to those Paul called "babes in Christ" (1 Cor 3:1). John noted two characteristics of little children. First, *their sins were forgiven*; that is, they had repented, believed the gospel, received forgiveness of sins, and were now children of God. Second, he said the children had *known the Father*. In other words, they had come to enjoy God as their heavenly Father. They were no longer orphans but, as children of God, were confident in the Father's love, delight, and acceptance. They were thrilled to be part of such a great family!

All believers start off as babes in Christ. When you're born again, the angels rejoice because God's family just got richer (Luke 15:10)!

But babes aren't very fruitful. For example, they don't contribute to the household budget. They don't help with the bills, pay the rent, or hold down a productive job. Babies are consumers. They eat a lot of food, fill a lot of diapers, go through lots of clothes, and require virtually incessant attention.

But while little children aren't fruitful contributors to the family budget, they're fruitful in another way: They bring gladness, laughter, and happiness to a family. They're just so stinkin' cute! Plus, they're packages of promise—that is, they embody a family's hopes and dreams for a promising future.

Similarly, *spiritual babes* are also consumers. They rarely do much to move the kingdom of God forward. Instead, they usually require lots of attention from more mature family members. They need a lot of prayer support, spiritual advice, coaching, wisdom, and fellowship. And they need teachers to constantly feed them the milk of the word. They take a lot without giving much in return. What they *do* give the family, however, is very important: joy, delight, and hope.

It's great to be a baby! It's just not great to stay a baby. If one of our children were to remain a baby for several years, we would be alarmed that something is seriously wrong. It's disturbing, similarly, when a spiritual babe remains a babe for a long time. Why? Because healthy babies grow.

Our heavenly Father rejoices over every babe, but He also wants them to mature and become young men.

Young Men

When John used the term *young men*, he wasn't being gender specific—that is, he wasn't writing to males only. Rather, he was pointing to a stage of spiritual maturity that is experienced by both genders.

John described three qualities of spiritual young men: They're strong, the word of God abides in them, and they've overcome the wicked one. Let's look at these.

First, they were strong—in spirit, mind, prayer, doctrine, perseverance, fervency, obedience, faith, love, conviction, devotion, etc. Second, the word of God was alive in them because they meditated in it day and night (Ps 1:2). No longer dependent on others to feed them the milk of the word, they had become self-feeders. As students of the word, they knew how to interpret the word and make it applicable to the lives of others (2 Tim 2:15; Heb 5:14). Third, the young men were effective in spiritual warfare. They had learned to resist temptation, overcome accusation, identify deception, and expose the devil's schemes. They were bold in prayer and strong in exploits.

Yes, young men are strong. If you want a job done, don't give it to a father, he's too tired. Give it to a young man with strong legs. Young men are ready to take on challenges that require energy, strength, and zeal. They're a force to be reckoned with. They'll organize and teach your training institute, launch your street evangelism outreach, lead your discipleship program, or build the infrastructure of your organization. They're stable, bold, and articulate. They're servant leaders. Young men and young women are the workhorses of the kingdom.

This second stage of fruitfulness is simply fantastic! Every Christian should aspire to become one of the *young men*. And yet, there's even more. There's fatherhood.

Fathers

John didn't mean the term *fathers* to be gender specific. He was referring to believers—whether male or female—who had matured to the third stage of spiritual fruitfulness.

John had only one thing to say about fathers: *You have known Him who is from the beginning.* Simply put, fathers have come to know God. Adversity has pressed them deeply into God, and through the course of their hardships, they've come to know the ways of God. For example, when Job finally saw God, he came to know that God "can do everything"

(Job 42:2). Fathers know God as their "faithful Creator" (1 Peter 4:19).

Knowing God is the great goal of every disciple. Paul's great aspiration was "that I may know Him" (Phil 3:10). Jesus said that knowing God was eternal life (John 17:3). Spiritual fathers know the Eternal One. This is the great desire of our hearts—to know God!

Fathers are veterans in the war with darkness, and they've got battle scars to show for it. They have a legacy of strong victories and abundant fruitfulness behind them. Yes, they've lost some battles, but even in those cases, their losses have produced their deepest growth and taught them how to be even more effective in the harvest.

Fathers have experienced hard things, darkness, loneliness, resistance, despondency, grief, affliction, betrayal, and loss. But through their struggles, they've come to know God in His eternity, omniscience, and omnipotence. Fathers help everyone find their place at the table, they maintain order in the house, and they provide an inheritance for the next generation.

Fathers are few (1 Cor 4:15). Believers are saved en masse, disciples are made in small groups, and fathers are fashioned in solitude.

No human can make a spiritual father. No university can crank out spiritual fathers. We can make disciples (Matt 28:19), but only God makes fathers. He makes them in John the Baptist deserts, or on lonely Abraham mountains, or in dry Moses wildernesses, or in wretched Joseph prisons.

Fathers bear much fruit. They seem to do so almost effortlessly, and this really amazes the young men. They can't figure it out. How can fathers be so fruitful with so little effort?

In contrast to fathers, young men seem to be working so much harder. They're juggling all kinds of balls and keeping everything operational. Young men are up early, laboring hard all day in the fields, and then late to bed. Sometimes, they feel like they're living on the edge of exhaustion.

And then a father strolls by.

He seems so chill. He's not panting or sweating, but the fruit from his life is remarkable in depth and significance. *How does he do it?* the young men wonder.

Fathers have learned that fruitfulness doesn't derive from working harder but from connectivity to the vine (John 15:5). Young men tend to serve God with their muscles and moxy, but fathers have come to serve God with their spirit (Rom 1:9). Fathers have found a realm of fruitfulness that is not attained by strength or talents or might or power, but by the Spirit of the Lord (Zech 4:6).

Fathers have discovered that abiding in Christ's love is the Master Key to fruitful living (John 15:9)

In their later years, spiritual fathers stop leading the charge and hand the baton for battle to the young men. The fathers might draw up the battle plans, but the young men execute the deployment (see 1 Kings 20:14). This gives the young men the experience they need to ultimately become spiritual fathers in their own right.

Three Stages of Fruitfulness

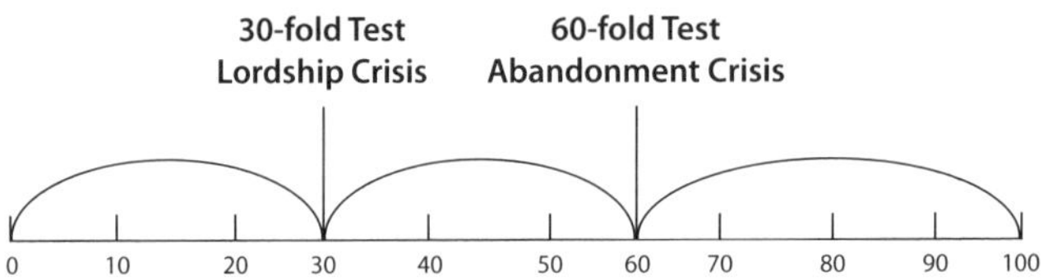

1 John 2:12-14	Children	Young Men	Fathers
Joseph	At Home	Potiphar's House	Palace
Moses	Pharaoh's House	Midian Wilderness	Israel's Leader
David	Shepherd	Captain	King
Jesus	Childhood	Earthly Ministry	Father's Right Hand

Examples of Three Stages

The life stories of several biblical characters divide naturally into three stages of maturity and fruitfulness. We'll mention the examples that are on Chart 2, as well as a few others.

Joseph. As already noted, he's one of the clearest examples in the Bible of three life stages. His thirtyfold years correspond to his teen years in his father's household. His sixtyfold years were his years of slavery, during which he managed all of Potiphar's operations and made Potiphar wealthy. His hundredfold fruitful years correspond to his reign in the palace, where he literally saved and sustained several nations in the region.

Jesus. His life divides easily into three stages. The first stage was His childhood and young adult years when His fruitfulness was mostly hidden. The second stage was His three years of ministry, at which time His fruitfulness grabbed the attention of all Israel. The third stage was His death, resurrection, and ascension to the Father, where He is now hundredfold fruitful at the Father's right hand.

Abraham. His first life stage was living in Ur of the Chaldees. His second stage was settling in Canaan. His third stage was launched when he offered his son Isaac on Mount Moriah. Because of his consecration at that altar, Abraham entered into the fruitfulness of true spiritual fatherhood.

David. He was thirtyfold fruitful as a shepherd in his father's house. Then, he was sixtyfold fruitful as a prince in Saul's army. Finally, he was hundredfold fruitful as king of Israel.

Moses. The three stages of Moses' life divide equally into forty-year periods. During his first forty years, Moses grew up in Pharaoh's house. In his second stage, he lived for forty years in the Midian wilderness where he was groomed by God for service. In his third forty-year stage, he led the nation of Israel from Egypt, through their grinding wilderness, to the border of Canaan.

Jacob. The three stages in Jacob's life are a bit fuzzy, but I think they can be seen. In stage one, he lived at home with his parents. In stage two, he lived in Haran with Laban's family. In stage three, he returned to Canaan where he nurtured the beginnings of the Israelite nation.

Job. For me, Job's life naturally divides into three stages. First were his years of initial serenity and prosperity. That was followed, in stage two, by many months in an agonizing trial. In his third stage, he enjoyed many years of restored blessing and profound spiritual fatherhood.

Paul. Paul's story seems to divide into three stages. In stage one, he grew up in Judaism. In stage two, after his conversion, he withdrew into obscurity for fourteen years of training in the Spirit. In stage three, he was brought by Barnabas to Antioch and launched into his public ministry.

Mordecai. In stage one, he raised Esther. In stage two, he sat in the king's gate and weathered the storm unleashed by Haman. In stage three, Mordecai demonstrated hundredfold fruitfulness by serving as second in command to King Ahasuerus and ruling over all the provinces of the Persian Empire (Esth 10:3).

Naomi. In her first stage, she lived with her family on their homestead in Bethlehem. In her second stage, she lived in Moab for ten years where she lost her husband and two sons. In stage three, she returned to Bethlehem where the Lord rewarded her with a redemption story (Ruth 4).

Zacharias. Stage one was his years of priestly service and barrenness. Stage two was his nine months of muteness and preparation for fatherhood. Stage three represented hundredfold fruitfulness, when he raised and prepared John the Baptist to serve as Christ's forerunner.

I'm sure there are others in the Bible whose life naturally divides into three stages of maturity, but with the above list we have strong evidence to support our thesis: *The life stories of many devout saints divide naturally into three stages of maturity or fruitfulness.*

This understanding may help you interpret your own

personal journey toward hundredfold fruitfulness—especially when you understand the two crisis points of transition. That's for our next chapter.

CHAPTER 22

Two Crisis Points

Three Stages of Fruitfulness

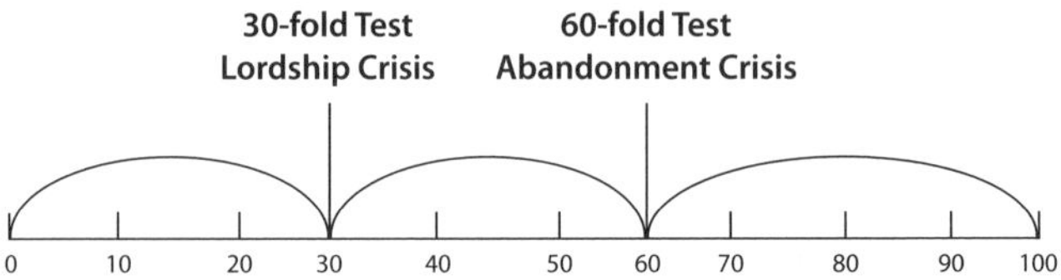

1 John 2:12-14	Children	Young Men	Fathers
Joseph	At Home	Potiphar's House	Palace
Moses	Pharaoh's House	Midian Wilderness	Israel's Leader
David	Shepherd	Captain	King
Jesus	Childhood	Earthly Ministry	Father's Right Hand

The journey of saints in Scripture often involved two crisis points. The second was more challenging, but then it opened to hundredfold fruitfulness.

Looking at Chart 2, the two crisis points are indicated at thirty and sixty. Each crisis leads to the next stage of fruitfulness. I call them *crisis points* because the dynamics within each transition often are—like many transitions in life—challenging.

Advancement involves struggle. For example, athletes in training know that gaining greater fitness involves pain. Similarly, maturing in fruitfulness typically involves struggle. At the two crisis points, the struggle can feel particularly intense.

I'm calling the thirtyfold crisis the *Lordship Crisis* because the issue for most believers at this threshold is submission to the Lordship of Christ. As our Lord, Christ calls us to die to self and take up the crucified life (Matt 16:24; Gal 2:20).

I'm calling the sixtyfold crisis the *Abandonment Crisis* because it sometimes involves a degree of abandonment to God's sovereignty that is more costly than we had anticipated.

Consider the example of Abraham. God led Abraham to a mountain where he actually had to bind his son Isaac, place him on the altar, and lift the knife (see Gen 22). God had given Abraham a living legacy, but Abraham never anticipated he would have to drive a dagger through it. God was testing Abraham to see if he would obey His voice even if he didn't understand the directive.

Imagine the emotions that must have coursed through Abraham's soul as he raised the knife to kill his only son. Fear, horror, perplexity, grief, dread, abhorrence. With tears flowing, he lifted his knife in obedience. Obedience! When Abraham let go of *everything*, he made it through the sixtyfold crisis. To pass the test required absolute abandonment to God's purposes.

The nature of these two crisis points are unique with every individual because God is remarkably creative in how He writes stories. No two are alike. Even so, we can draw encouragement from the stories of others. When we examine these two crisis points in the lives of biblical characters and see God's goodness in enlarging their fruitfulness, we gain courage for our own pilgrimage.

Perhaps the best way to understand the nature of these two crisis points is to consider real life examples from Scripture. Let's look, therefore, at the two crisis points as they seemed to occur in the lives of the biblical characters we mentioned last chapter.

Examples of Two Crisis Points

Joseph. His first crisis was enslavement—when his brothers sold him into slavery. Because of his honorable response to their rejection, he stepped into sixtyfold fruitfulness in Potiphar's house. His faithfulness in Potiphar's house qualified him for his second crisis point: prison. That second crisis (wrongful incarceration) was much more agonizing than the first (slavery). For nearly ten years, he was buried in a foul Egyptian prison. He responded redemptively to that test too, however, and consequently qualified to enter into hundredfold fruitfulness. Raised to the throne of Egypt, his hundredfold fruitfulness was demonstrated in four remarkable ways: (1) He saved the lives of every individual in Egypt, (2) he became a feeder of nations, (3) he made Pharaoh the richest man on the planet, and best of all, (4) he established his family in prosperity in the land of Goshen where they could grow into a nation (see Gen 37-47).

Jesus. His first crisis point came at His forty-day temptation in the wilderness. When He passed that test, He entered into the sixtyfold fruitfulness of His earthly ministry. But a bigger test was yet to come—the cross. The cross was Jesus' second crisis point, and He navigated it through utter abandonment to His Father's purpose. Although a horrific struggle, Calvary was the crossing that enabled Him to step over into the highest fruitfulness. He now sits at the Father's right hand where He is hundredfold fruitful and is bringing together His Father's eternal plan for our entire planet.

Abraham. His first crisis was to leave the familiarity of Ur and depart for a land he didn't know. But the greater crisis was yet to come—the offering of his only begotten son, Isaac, on Mount Moriah (see Gen 22). As he lifted the knife over his son, he abandoned all his hopes and dreams in sheer obedience to the voice of God. When he passed that test, He received from heaven the most profuse blessing imaginable, became the father of the faithful, and proved himself a friend of God.

David. His thirtyfold crisis was his skirmish with Goliath (see 1 Sam 17). When he passed that faith test by killing the giant, he entered into sixtyfold fruitfulness as a captain in Saul's army. But the greater test was yet to come—years of banishment as he ran for his life from Saul. When that sixtyfold test was finally over, David was crowned king and enjoyed decades of hundredfold fruitfulness as the monarch of Israel.

Moses. When Moses was forty, he defended a fellow Israelite, and consequently, Pharaoh tried to kill him. Moses had to run for his life. This ouster from the palace was the first crisis point in Moses' life. The second crisis came when he was eighty. God visited him in a burning bush and conscripted him to lead the nation of Israel out of Egypt (see Exod 3). When Moses accepted that call, he crossed over into hundredfold fruitfulness. In the final forty years of his life, he led the nation of Israel out of Egypt, through the wilderness, and to the border of Canaan.

Jacob. His brother Esau intended to kill him, so Jacob left home for Haran (see Gen 28). That departure from all that was familiar was his thirtyfold crisis. In Haran, Jacob entered into sixtyfold fruitfulness as he grew his family and wealth base. His sixtyfold crisis came when, on his way home from Haran, he wrestled all night with the Angel of the Lord (see Gen 32). The encounter was so intense he came away with a permanent limp. Jacob limped his way into hundredfold fruitfulness, blessed Pharaoh, and saw his family established in prosperity in the land of Goshen.

Job. I struggle to identify what might have been Job's first crisis. Perhaps it was when his adult children wandered from the heritage of his spiritual legacy. Whatever it might have been, his second crisis is abundantly clear because that's the storyline of his book. The book of Job is an expansive, forty-two-chapter treatise on the Abandonment Crisis. When he came through that crisis redemptively, Job entered into hundredfold fruitfulness—true spiritual fatherhood in the faith (see Job 42).

Mordecai. Mordecai's thirtyfold crisis was possibly connected to the difficulties that caused him to bring Esther into his home and raise her. The book of Esther focuses primarily, however, on his sixtyfold crisis. Out of spite for Mordecai, Haman devised a plan to exterminate Mordecai's entire people group—the Jews—who were spread throughout the

Persian Empire. Mordecai responded redemptively to this agonizing crisis and, consequently, advanced into hundredfold fruitfulness as the second ruler over the entire Empire (see Esther 10).

Naomi. Naomi's first crisis point was when she and her family, under the duress of a terrible famine, forsook their Bethlehem homestead and fled to Moab. Her second crisis point was when she lost her husband and two sons (see Ruth 1). Their deaths were devastating, but when Naomi responded redemptively to the Lord's crushing, she eventually stepped into hundredfold fruitfulness as great-grandmother to the Davidic Dynasty.

Zacharias. I'd identify his first crisis as childlessness (his wife Elizabeth was barren), and his second crisis as muteness (God struck him mute for disbelieving Gabriel's message). When Zacharias endured the Lord's chastening, he entered into hundredfold fruitfulness—fathering the great prophet John the Baptist (see Luke 1-2).

These examples seem to support our thesis: *The journey of saints in Scripture often involved two crisis points, with the second opening to hundredfold fruitfulness.*

The Lordship Crisis

My tags for the two great crisis points of a saint's pilgrimage are the *Lordship Crisis* and the *Abandonment Crisis*. Both involve death to self, but the second excavates the heart more deeply.

First, let me say a few things about the Lordship Crisis. It's an invitation to the crucified life. The Lord will invite us to surrender everything to Him—our strength, time, will, resources, desires, and aspirations. Up to this point, we may have been self-determining in our life goals, but He will crucify our self-determination and invite us to bow to His purposes for our lives.

In one sense, the Lordship Crisis is a Faith Crisis. We wonder, *If I surrender everything to Christ, will it end well? Will my life be hindered or enhanced? Does it really pay to give Jesus an unqualified yes?* Our confidence in His goodness is being tested.

For example, we wonder what He might take from us if we give Him total Lordship. Will He place us in a career we don't enjoy? Will He send us to a nation where our daily living is miserable? Will we live in loneliness or abject poverty for the rest of our lives?

When we surrender to His Lordship at the thirtyfold crisis, we often find ourselves surprised that, instead of taking something precious from us, He adds amazing blessings to us. He's so pleased with our consecration that He lavishes His pleasure on us, quiets our hearts with His love, and brings us into greater fulfillment than we anticipated. Rather than crushing our dreams, He leads us into levels of fruitfulness that fulfill our dreams. We find ourselves thinking, *This is why I was created! Saying yes to the cross leads to the most satisfying life of fruitfulness possible!* We say with David, "The lines have fallen to me in pleasant places; yes, I have a good inheritance" (Ps 16:6).

At the thirtyfold crisis, we're established in the confidence that He is good and it's safe to give Him our wholehearted *yes*. As we cross this threshold, new vistas open to us. We experience fresh momentum, purpose, fruitfulness. We thrill in the holy adventure of Galatians 2:20, "I have been crucified with Christ; it is no longer I who live, but Christ lives in me; and the life which I now live in the flesh I live by faith in the Son of God, who loved me and gave Himself for me."

We think to ourselves, *I've just passed the greatest test of my walk with Christ!* True, it's the greatest test you've known to date, but there's likely an even greater test coming. You've passed the Lordship Crisis but have yet to pass the Abandonment Crisis.

The Abandonment Crisis

Let me say a couple things about the Abandonment Crisis. Job referred to it when he wrote, "The LORD gave, and the LORD has taken away; blessed be the name of the LORD" (Job 1:21).

At the thirtyfold crisis, you gave it all to Him, only to discover that instead of taking it all from you, He gave you even more. But the sixtyfold crisis is different. This time, when you give it all to Him, He actually takes it.

It's easy to serve God when He gives; the challenge comes when He takes away.

The sixtyfold Abandonment Crisis typically involves significant losses, and comes in many forms and settings. It can look like Joseph's prison, or Jesus' cross, or David's cave, or Naomi's bereavement, or Abraham's knife, or Job's crucible. It can involve financial ruin, or physical suffering, or relational conflict, or in some cases (like Job and Jesus) all three.

In the next chapter, we're going to examine some of the emotional elements that can accompany the sixtyfold Abandonment Crisis.

CHAPTER 23

Emotional Elements of the Sixtyfold Crisis

In the sixtyfold Abandonment Crisis, when we feel like we're being crushed, we can look to the great cloud of witnesses and glean from their testimonies (see Heb 12:1). Their experiences help us understand God's ways so that, instead of losing heart, we can endure in obedience and overcome.

Intense emotional swings can accompany the sixtyfold crisis. I'll mention some of the common emotional elements experienced by some of the witnesses who went before us.

Wilderness

Those who navigated the sixtyfold crisis in Scripture often felt like they were walking through a *wilderness.* Wilderness-like seasons commonly include some of the following elements:

- Unbelief is purged (Ezek 20:35-38).
- There's a painful disconnect between the promises you hold and the land you inhabit. For example, when Israel was in their forty-year wilderness, they held promises of inheriting the verdant land of Canaan, but the land they were actually inhabiting was pure desert.
- Your sense of being fruitful is shut down.
- You're carried along by God (Deut 1:31).
- The anointing on your life is stronger than your current responsibilities (1 Sam 16:13).

- You're in preparation for your next assignment (Exod 2:15-3:1).
- You're experiencing supernatural preservation (Neh 9:41).
- You find moments of uncommon intimacy with God (Jer 2:2; Hos 2:14-16; 13:5).
- You learn a new cadence in your stride with God (Ps 68:7).
- Your sustenance is a daily miracle (Exod 16:31).
- You're being prepared to kill the giants in your promised land.

The deflated emotions of the wilderness are challenging to navigate, but they open to unprecedented conquests of promise.

Loneliness

Loneliness is a common experience for saints in the sixtyfold crisis. For example, Jesus experienced profound loneliness on the cross. Not only did His disciples forsake Him, but His Father did, too (Ps 22:1). Jesus had to experience loneliness so He could help us with ours. When you bring your loneliness to Him, you're coming to Someone who understands.

When Jacob navigated his sixtyfold crisis, he was *left alone* so He could wrestle with Jesus through the night (Gen 32:24). In this dark night of the soul, it's just you and Jesus.

In the loneliness, God dries up your dependence on other social sources until He alone is the fountain of your heart (see Hos 2:14). The loneliness is designed to bring you into friendship with God. He'll show you how, when necessary, to get your social needs met in Christ alone. He'll take you through loneliness so you'll be equipped to navigate the unique terrain of hundredfold fruitfulness.

God uses loneliness redemptively in our lives, but I don't believe He intends to leave us there permanently. He created us for companionship and fellowship (Gen 2:18). Loneliness is a formative tool that is useful in His hands, but His intention is to bring us through into hundredfold fruitfulness among the throngs of God's people (Ps 142:7). When we come through, the holy abandonment we gained to God's purposes will stay with us.

For those who experience the loss of children, you may be stunned with the way the Lord once again surrounds you with many children (Isa 49:21).

When a grain of wheat falls into the ground and dies, it dies *all alone*. But don't despise the loneliness, because the lonely death is prerequisite to the abundant fruitfulness that follows (John 12:24).

Despondency

Despondency is a common emotional feeling for those in the Abandonment Crisis, and here's why. This crisis usually involves some form of loss, and loss naturally leads to feelings of grief. Grief, in turn, sometimes produces feelings of despondency.

I've experienced this personally. In my own journey, I endured a fifteen-year battle with depression. I write about it in my book *Unrelenting Prayer*. Here's something I learned: Part of the struggle with despondency is to be resisted, and part is to be harnessed. Let me explain.

There's an element in despondency to be resisted—the demonic element. When you're imprisoned with purpose by the hand of God, the devil will try to take advantage of your weakness and bury your soul under a mountain of discouragement. When struggling with despondency, therefore, some of it is probably demonically incited. How do we fight that? We "resist the devil" (James 4:7)! Don't just lay down and surrender to the enemy's devices. Rather, gather a few spiritual friends to fight and resist with you. Ask them to stand with you in prayer, and reinforce a perimeter of holy fire around your life so the enemy has to back off and keep his distance.

After the enemy has been pushed back, you'll probably feel a sense of reprieve, but yet there may not be a complete lifting of the despondency. Why not? Because there may be an element in your depression that God is using to *train* you. Some muscle groups in the Spirit are not exercised apart from despondency. Just as the resistance of weights helps a weightlifter to bulk up, the resistance of your emotional despondency can be harnessed to make you stronger than ever for the fruitfulness that's coming. Respond properly to despondency and you'll emerge from the trial with might in the Spirit—like David's mighty men—for greater exploits.

Perplexity

The saint in the sixtyfold crisis often encounters profound perplexity about God and His ways. Things they thought they knew about God sometimes become foggy and uncertain. God's purpose is that the perplexity form a greater dependence on Him for every step.

For example, when Abraham was being taken through his Abandonment Crisis, God told him to sacrifice his son, Isaac. That directive was contrary to everything Abraham thought he knew about God. After all, God had said to Noah, "Whoever sheds man's blood, by man his blood shall be shed; for in the image of God He made man" (Gen 9:6). Abraham was probably thinking, *If I kill Isaac, my friends will have to kill me. Everything will be lost!*

Abraham was caught in the vise grip of perplexity. *How can I kill my son when God has proscribed murder? What should I do? Should I disobey the voice or kill my son?*

Torn by perplexity, Abraham somehow made the right decision: He obeyed the Voice. And here's how God responded:

> **"By Myself I have sworn, says the LORD, because you have done this thing, and have not withheld your son, your only son—blessing I will bless you, and multiplying I will multiply your descendants as the stars of the heaven and as the sand which is on the seashore; and your descendants shall possess the gate of their enemies. In your seed all the nations of the earth shall be blessed, because you have obeyed My voice" (Gen 22:16-18).**

God blew Abraham's theological grid. Don't be overly surprised, therefore, if God steps outside the confines of your theology and does something you thought He would never do. Through the perplexity, you'll come to know Him more deeply and personally than ever. And get this from Abraham's example: Always follow the Voice!

Ecclesiological Crisis

The saint in the sixtyfold crisis sometimes experiences an ecclesiological crisis. *Ecclesiological* is a fancy adjective that means the matter is related to the church. In this *ecclesiological crisis,* the pilgrim sometimes experiences strong struggles in their relationships within the church—that is, with leaders and members of the body of Christ.

For example, Job's relationships with his three best friends became painfully vexing during his trial. His friends were trying to serve with "helpful perspective," but their flawed discernment only added to the strain on his soul. He refused to turn away from them, however. Even though their accusations and rejection assaulted his soul, he continued to walk with them in humility because he perceived their role in his trial was ordained of God.

Take a tip from Job. If you find yourself in the Abandonment Crisis, don't step away from the church or remove yourself from Christian fellowship. Even though they might reject you, continue to walk with them, as much as lies within you.

Why should you stay? Because it's within the environs of the church you'll find your salvation. Jesus is very intentional in expressing His kingdom through His church. We see this, for example, in Paul's acclamation, "Now to Him who is able to do exceedingly abundantly above all that we ask or think, according to the power that works in us, to Him be glory in the church by Christ Jesus to all generations, forever and ever. Amen" (Eph 3:20-21). God has designed that glory should always come to Him *in the church* by Christ Jesus.

Even when relationships get hard, remain in fellowship with believers so that God might be glorified through your life.

Wilderness, loneliness, despondency, perplexity, relational crisis—all these challenges are intensely emotional in nature. If you experience some of these emotions, could it be that God is taking you through an Abandonment Crisis in order to bring you into hundredfold fruitfulness?

In the next chapter, I want to emphasize just one more thing about the sixtyfold crisis.

CHAPTER 24

This Is the Big One

Three Stages of Fruitfulness

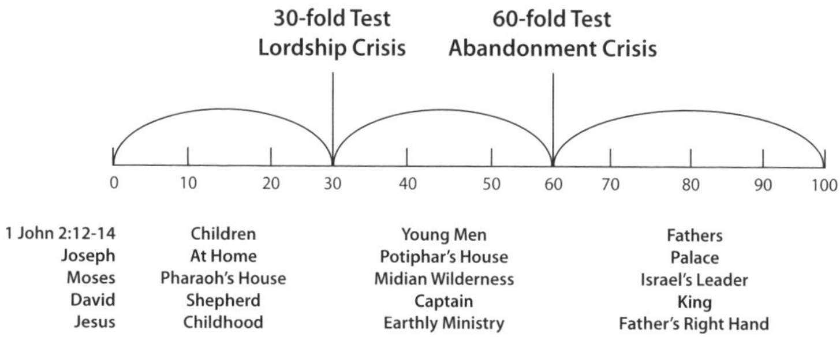

This chapter simply emphasizes that the sixtyfold crisis is *the big one*. I mean, it's typically the biggest crisis of your Christian pilgrimage. All of us experience many trials in our journey, but the sixtyfold crisis is most intense of all. Once you navigate it successfully, the realms of fruitfulness that lie beyond will truly be remarkable and delightful.

It's helpful to understand this about the sixtyfold crisis: The intensity of the trial seems disproportionately severe to the issues in your soul that need to change. Yes, you know you have issues that need to change, but the intensity of the fire feels like overkill. Keep this in mind, though: The fire of the trial isn't this intense because God is targeting your issues; it's intense because God is rewriting your spiritual DNA. This intensity is normative to the sixtyfold crisis. He's qualifying you for something. He's excavating your heart more deeply right now than you can understand. It's this intense because He's training you for hundredfold fruitfulness. The deeper the excavation, the more abundant the subsequent harvest.

Endure! Run this race all the way to the finish.

Take another look at Chart 2. The thirtyfold crisis is a lesser trial, and the sixtyfold crisis is a greater trial. This was true for Jesus—the cross was more intense than His forty-day temptation. This was also true for Joseph—His imprisonment was tougher than his slavery. The same was true of Abraham—the altar where he offered his son as a burnt offering was more agonizing than the earlier test of leaving his home in Ur of the Chaldees. In each case, the second one was the big one. This may also be true for you.

When you're in the sixtyfold crisis, you may feel forsaken by God and betrayed by friends. The struggle and warfare may be intense and unremitting. You may lose favor, reputation, status, title, and office. You may lose your following and your income stream. You may lose all hope of ever being fruitful again. "Like a wineskin in smoke," you may feel as though the fire has ruined you (Ps 119:83). Yes, this is the big one. This is the test that will determine whether you become a casualty or abandoned to God's will and more fruitful than ever.

If the Lord cuts you off in your youth, don't relinquish hope. Jeremiah wrote, "It is good for a man to bear the yoke in his youth" (Lam 3:27). In the language of our parable, Jeremiah was saying that it's good for a man to go through the sixtyfold crisis in his youth. In other words, it's better to navigate the Abandonment Crisis when you're young rather than when you're elderly and approaching the end of your race. Why? Because after you've overcome, you'll still have some years of hundredfold fruitfulness before you. It's better, therefore, to navigate the two great crisis points of the Christian life earlier rather than later in life.

The idea that there are two crisis points in the life of a believer seems to be confirmed in the journey of the Bride of Christ in the Song of Solomon. That book follows the Bride on an eight-chapter journey that culminates in hundredfold fruitfulness. Her thirtyfold crisis is found in Song 3:1-5, where she learns obedience to the Bridegroom. Her sixtyfold crisis is found in Song 5:1 to 6:3, and is much more intense.

In that second crisis, the Bride is tested both by losing her awareness of the Lord's presence and by being misunderstood and hurt by the body of Christ. She walks redemptively through both crises, however, and eventually attains the hundredfold fruitfulness of Song 8:12, "My own vineyard is before me. You, O Solomon, may have a thousand, and those who tend its fruit two hundred."

Not All Pass the Thirtyfold Test

The thirtyfold Lordship test is the lesser test, but not all believers successfully cross that threshold and move beyond thirtyfold fruitfulness. Why not? Because of birds, stones, and weeds.

In other words, they said *no* to God somewhere in the journey. They may not even have it clearly identified in their consciousness, but there was a moment when they declined an invitation from the Holy Spirit to greater consecration. And He honored their response. Perhaps they hung back, postponed, resisted, overlooked, dismissed, neglected, or disregarded the Lord's invitation to obedience. Perhaps the cost was too high, the knife too sharp, the cross too demanding, the call too unsavory, the self-denial too severe. It wasn't a heaven-or-hell issue. When they declined the invitation, their name wasn't removed from the Book of Life. It was a consecration issue—whether or not they would step forward into greater obedience and fruitfulness.

In accordance with the trampled heart, perhaps the Lord wanted them to stop allowing their heart to be trampled by beasts, but they were unwilling. Or in accordance with the shallow heart, perhaps there was a stone of sinful compromise they were unwilling to remove. Or in accordance with the neglected heart, perhaps there was an encroaching weed they chose to tolerate rather than cut back. They allowed some kind of hindrance to remain in the garden of their heart and, consequently, were unable to enjoy greater fruitfulness.

Some saints seem to camp at a certain level of fruitfulness and just hang there for years. Year after year, they seem to circle around the same general level of fruitfulness. After twenty years, not much has changed. They still love Jesus and they're still in the kingdom, but their fruitfulness has not increased with the years. In such instances, what's going on? What's the hindrance? Why haven't they progressed to greater fruitfulness? Because of birds, stones, or weeds. It may be because they were unwilling to embrace the cost of the thirtyfold test.

The point is, only *some* believers pass the thirtyfold test.

Not All Pass the Sixtyfold Test

And secondly, only some believers pass the sixtyfold Abandonment Crisis. What I mean is, there are some who successfully cross the thirtyfold barrier and continue to grow in fruitfulness, but when they come to the sixtyfold crisis, they stop and camp there.

Not all believers are offered the sixtyfold test. Why not? My understanding here is very small. From my limited perspective, it seems that some believers don't enter the Abandonment Crisis because *they don't ask for it*.

There are some things in the kingdom for which you must ask. There are places with Christ you'll never walk until you pray the dangerous prayer and sing the dangerous song.

Jesus asked for it. The Father's invitation was, "Ask of Me, and I will give You the nations for Your inheritance, and the ends of the earth for Your possession" (Ps 2:8). So Jesus asked. He asked His Father for the nations, and it meant the sixtyfold crisis—the cross.

Job asked for it. Job wrote, "I am one mocked by his friends, who called on God, and He answered him, the just and blameless who is ridiculed" (Job 12:4). Job was saying, "I asked God for something, He answered my prayer, and now my friends mock and ridicule me." This has us wondering, *Job, what did you ask for?* Job didn't say, but he did tell us he prayed a dangerous prayer that precipitated his ordeal.

What are dangerous prayers? Prayers that are so trusting in God's generosity that they give Him a blank slate to write the story His way.

What do dangerous prayers sound like? Well, okay, I will tell you the dangerous prayer: *Whatever it takes.*

That prayer is dangerous because it's willing to pay any price to enter into greater kingdom fruitfulness.

I've got to have You, God—whatever it takes.

I've got to know You, Jesus—whatever it takes.

I've got to see You, Jesus—whatever it takes.

I've got to be closer, Lord—whatever it takes.

I need more of Your love and power—whatever it takes.

I've got to have my family for the kingdom, Lord—whatever it takes.

That prayer is so lovesick and abandoned to His providence that it hands Jesus a blank check. *Jesus, I invite You to do whatever it takes to get me where I need to be. I can't get there on my own, so I surrender fully to Your leadership in my life. I know that the path You choose will be perfect. I'm confident in Your goodness, mercy, and grace. Do whatever it takes, but give me more of You!*

When you're desperate and abandoned enough to pray the dangerous prayer—in sincerity, faith, and love—that's the kind of praying that can get you unstuck and moving forward again toward hundredfold fruitfulness.

CHAPTER 25

Two Personal Stories

I'll close by telling how I connect personally with the thirtyfold and sixtyfold crisis points. As I share my stories, my first story is going to date me, but I believe the Lord will strengthen your faith in His good purposes for your own journey.

My Thirtyfold Lordship Crisis

When I was twenty-two years old, I finished a year of study at Evangel University in Springfield, Missouri, and transferred to Elim Bible Institute in Lima, New York. I sensed a call to vocational ministry and felt that a Bible College like Elim would help prepare me for that calling.

It was 1979, and at that time Elim had a lot of rules and restrictions for their students because the leaders wanted the school to be a place of spiritual formation and holy consecration in preparation for servant leadership. They had rules regarding dress because the virtues of modesty, propriety, and self-control were valued. For example, shorts were restricted exclusively to the dorms or gym and couldn't be worn anywhere else on campus.

They had a dress code for chapels and classes. In those contexts, women were required to wear uniform skirts, and men had to wear a sports jacket and tie. Jeans were unacceptable in classes and chapels. Elim has since relaxed their dress code requirements for students, but in 1979 the rules were rather strict.

I was doing okay with the dress code requirements until the day they called a special men's meeting in order to announce a new rule. They announced that corduroy pants were now also forbidden in classes and chapels. They explained that some of the corduroy pants being worn to classes by some of the men were too worn and sloppy. I've since wondered if it were maybe *my* corduroy pants that triggered this new rule, because corduroys were my primary means of dress for classes and some of my pairs were probably well-worn.

That restriction hit me real hard. To tell you why, I need to explain something rather personal.

I have a weird skin sensitivity. It's almost like a skin allergy. There are certain fabrics that cause my skin to itch. For example, if I wear wool or polyester on my skin, it feels like I have insects crawling on my body. Cotton, on the other hand, is great for me. I can wear cotton products like jeans and corduroys without a problem.

Back in 1979, polyester was the rage. Almost all the pants sold in stores were made of polyester and synthetic blends. It was almost impossible to find pants for men made of cotton. It's different today. For example, Dockers are just one kind of cotton-based pants that are widely available today. They iron well and look nice. But back in 1979, cotton materials such as Dockers and khakis did not yet exist.

In the 1980s, the textiles industry advanced, and manufacturers found new ways to weave cotton into men's clothing. Today it's easy for me to find cotton pants, but in 1979 those materials were not yet developed. Consequently, back in the 1970s I wore jeans and corduroys a lot.

With the new rule in 1979, I could wear neither jeans nor corduroys to classes. My wardrobe was instantly reduced to just one pair of pants that met the rules and that didn't itch. I had to wear that same pair of pants to every class and every chapel service, every day of the week. And it wasn't as though I could go to the mall and buy more pants, even though I tried. Virtually all the pants in the stores that satisfied Elim's rules itched me.

I was at an impasse. I didn't know what I would wear anymore, but more than that, I was totally annoyed by the new rule. It seemed so petty and picayune. What's more, it rankled my pride. Let me explain the ego part.

After high school, I worked hard for years at labor-intensive jobs in order to save up for college. My parents couldn't afford to send me to college, so I earned and paid my own way. I paid my year at Evangel, and now I was paying my way at Elim. I owned a little Chevette car that I had bought with my own hard-earned money, I was working part-time while enrolled in school full-time, I was twenty-two years old, and I was making my own way forward in life. I was a man—hard-working, financially responsible, sober-minded, self-motivated, and pressing into the upward call of God in Christ. But they were treating me like a three-year-old. I was so annoyed by the new, insulting rule that I almost packed up and left.

I didn't know what to do, and I needed to talk to God about it. I found an empty dorm room in Watson Hall, knelt before a hardback chair, and said, *God, they're treating me like a three-year-old!* It all seemed so demeaning and unwarranted to me. *Should I just leave?*

As I knelt in prayer, I seemed to sense the Lord asking, *Are you willing to be treated like a three-year-old?*

Here I was—a self-determining, self-sufficient, self-supporting twenty-two-year-old, laboring with all my strength to find my place vocationally in life and ministry. But I sensed the Lord putting His finger on my pride and self-determination. Was I willing to humble myself, submit to the new rule, and let them treat me like a three-year-old? It's difficult to convey just how painful that question was for me at the time. At twenty-two, I was devoting all my strength to finding and establishing my maturity and manhood. *Be treated like a three-year-old?* The question was driving the cross straight through my heart. The possibility of submitting to the humiliating rule was literally killing me.

Kneeling at that chair, I bawled like a baby. I could hold to my pride and leave the school, or I could crucify my pride and surrender to the new rule. Tears flowed while I did business with God.

Finally, I prayed, *Okay, Lord, they can treat me like a three-year-old.* The cross went through my heart like a dagger, and something about my self-life died in that moment. The demise was excruciating. That altar was so painful that I've never forgotten it. I rose from my knees and quietly donned the new, idiotic, insulting rule.

At the time, I didn't realize how significant that altar was. But in later years I came to realize it was my thirtyfold test. It was my Lordship Crisis. It was a real, tangible, painful surrender to the cross. I chose to die to self, take up my cross, and follow Jesus. Looking back, I realize God was crucifying my prideful self-determination and calling me to a deeper surrender.

From that day of surrender, I moved forward in fruitfulness in God. His favor shone on my life, and I slowly walked toward thirty-onefold, thirty-twofold—into increasing fruitfulness. I sincerely believe that, at age twenty-two, I crossed the thirtyfold barrier.

When I said *yes* to the crucified life, I thought the big test was behind me. What I didn't realize was that a much greater test was yet before me.

My Sixtyfold Abandonment Crisis

I graduated from Elim Bible Institute in May of 1981, at a time when the presiding Music Director—my big brother—was leaving to further his education. That summer, Elim asked me to replace my brother Sheldon as the Music Director. That was a significant summer for me: Bible school graduation, marriage, and a new role as Music Director at the school. I was moving forward in fruitfulness.

In 1986, I accepted a call to serve as lead pastor of a local church in the Rochester, New York area called Zion Fellowship.

We pastored that church for thirteen years. Through those years, I progressed toward sixtyfold fruitfulness.

After pastoring for six years, everything changed. In 1992, I suffered a debilitating vocal injury. At first, it simply seemed to be a sore throat. But in May of 1992, it developed into something more. It felt like I had a marble lodged in my throat. The doctor diagnosed it as a *contact ulcer* on the left arytenoid. The arytenoids are two cartilages that bring the vocal cords together to sound. When I felt the marble in my throat, I could tell something was seriously wrong.

Vocal rest didn't improve anything, and steroids seemed to make it worse. Eventually, after much prayer, in August of 1992 I followed my doctor's advice and had laser surgery to remove the ulcer. The doctor assured me I'd be back in the pulpit in three weeks.

The surgery removed the ulcer but did something else. Something went wrong, and we still don't know exactly what was botched. My best guess is that the laser was used too aggressively or imprecisely and hit some nerves. Whatever went wrong, since then I have chronic pain when speaking and maybe 5 percent of my vocal strength. Every word hurts.

Words fail to express the intensity of this fiery trial. It's been harder than anything I ever imagined would come my way. I've suffered profound losses in almost every area of life. For starters, I've suffered losses with my children—because I was unable to communicate adequately with them during their formative years. The emotional availability that children need is supplied through *words*—conversation—and that was precisely what I was physically incapable of providing. I was affectionate and present physically, but I couldn't fill their need for a dad who was emotionally available to them.

I've also suffered professional losses. I had to relinquish the ministry of worship leading. Eventually, I had to resign my function as a lead pastor because I could no longer maintain leadership team cohesiveness. To explain, teams are galvanized and kept together through the glue of *words*—a commodity I could no longer provide. Consequently, my team of primary leaders became unglued from my leadership. I possessed the skills to build team cohesiveness but had lost the physical ability to exercise those skills.

I've also suffered relational losses. I've been separated from people that I thought would be lifelong friends and lifelong partners in ministry. Maintaining meaningful friendships has been one of the greatest challenges throughout this fiery ordeal.

Mind you, not everything has been a loss. In a moment, I'll mention some of the wonderful things I've gained in this journey. But right now, I'm being transparent about the intensity of the losses. In addition to physical, emotional, and relational pain, I've also endured substantial theological pain. I didn't understand how I could be loving God, serving Him, obeying Him, growing in fruitfulness, and then suffer a hit that took me out of everything He had called me to. My theology told me that "the gifts and callings of God are irrevocable" (Rom 11:29), but now I was losing everything He had called me to—pastoring people and leading worship. I didn't have a theology for a God who takes. I knew the God who gives, but I didn't know the God who takes away (Job 1:21).

The bad surgery plunged me into emotional darkness. I walked around in a numb, dark fog. Would I awaken one day and realize it was just a bad dream? But no, it wasn't a passing dream, it was a nightmare from which I couldn't escape.

I know Scripture says we shouldn't think of our fiery trial as though something strange was happening to us (1 Pet 4:12), but my trial seemed really weird. None of my peers seemed to be going through something this intense. I felt like a "spectacle" (1 Cor 4:9). I felt reproach from others. Some of the reproach was real, and some was imagined. I believed and preached the healing power of Christ, but struggled to find faith to access His healing power for myself.

I didn't know it in 1992, but I had stepped into my sixtyfold test. This was the Abandonment Crisis. Would my heart be abandoned to Christ, no matter how grievous the trial? Would I continue to praise Him for His goodness and give Him my wholehearted love, or would I get offended and succumb to accusation? The test has been intense on steroids.

My Dangerous Song

A few months after the bad surgery, while I was engulfed in blackness, a sister in our church paused one Sunday morning as she was leaving the sanctuary and stopped to say, "You asked God for something, and He has answered your prayer." Then she continued to exit the building.

I had no idea what that meant, but something about it seemed to ring true. But if it was true, then I was in trouble because that meant I was in a journey with God that I had asked for. If this was a God-journey, then it likely wouldn't be over in a couple minutes. It seemed that I was strapped to a story that God was writing.

What did I ask for? I couldn't remember.

I made that question a matter of prayer. *Lord, did I ask You for something? And if I did, what was it? When was it? What did I say? I need You to remind me, because I don't remember asking for something.*

In His kindness, the Lord reminded me of a prayer I had offered a few months earlier but then forgotten. I'll tell you about it.

It was my custom in those days to come early in the mornings to the building of the church I was pastoring, in order be with Jesus and pray. The church sanctuary was my secret place. I would sit at the piano, place my open Bible on the music stand, and sing to the Lord from Scripture. The Lord reminded me about one of those mornings.

On a certain morning, I was playing the piano and singing from Scripture. As I prayed, a certain hymn came to mind that I knew from childhood. I sang the hymn to the Lord, and the tears started. The song was giving language to a cry deep within my heart.

The hymn's lyrics go like this:

> Lord, lift me up and let me stand
> By faith on heaven's tableland
> A higher plane than I have found
> Lord, plant my feet on higher ground[1]

I wept because of a deep dissatisfaction in my soul. True, there were tokens of increasing fruitfulness in my life. For example, I had written a well-received book *(Exploring Worship)* and was pastoring a growing church. But there was a deep cry in my heart for greater fruitfulness. When I read the life and ministry of Jesus in the Gospels, I saw Him moving in dimensions of love, power, and authority such as I had never touched. He said we would do even greater works than His, but my works weren't even close to His. When I read about the power and intimacy He had with the Father, I knew He came to make the same available to me. But my level of experience wasn't even close to His. Oh, how my soul longed to move in the power of God like Jesus did.

But how could I possibly touch it? If rising to that higher ground meant working harder, I knew I could never attain it. Why not? Because I was already working as hard as I possibly could. I was thirty-five years old, in my prime, and I was giving the work of the ministry every ounce of my strength. I was up early to pray and to bed late at night because of ministry responsibilities. I simply couldn't work any harder. I was running as hard as I could possibly run and had nothing more to give. Even though I was giving the kingdom my all,

---

1 Johnson Oatman, Jr, "Higher Ground," 1898.

I looked at the fruit of my life and ministry and realized that my experience was far below what Jesus modeled.

There was a higher place, but I couldn't get there in my own strength. I realized that I needed help. I needed the Lord to *lift me* to a higher plane. That's why the lyrics of the hymn connected so viscerally with me in that moment. *Lord, lift me up!*

I wept openly as I cried to God to lift me to a higher plane.

The next morning, it happened all over again. Same place, same time, same piano, same song, same tears, same reach, same cry. I asked for the same thing two days in a row.

And then I forgot about it.

But God didn't forget. He heard my dangerous prayer, and I believe in His sovereign kindness He decided to say yes. He opened a door and took me on a journey. The catalyst was a vocal injury; the purpose was to lead me to a higher place. A place that is higher than sixtyfold fruitfulness. A place that opens to hundredfold fruitfulness. A place of greater love, greater intimacy, greater understanding, greater authority, and greater power. In other words, greater fruitfulness.

This is the journey I'm on, still today. I haven't attained the higher plane for which my soul yearns, but I'm higher in the foothills than I used to be. And by God's grace, I trust He'll continue to lift me higher.

You're Coming Higher!

I view this trial as my sixtyfold test.[2] In this trial, I've fought fiercely with depression, loneliness, and the lies of the deceiver. The infirmity looms before me like a great mountain. Sometimes all I can see are the things that I *can't* do. For example, I can't talk, can't sing, can't lead or function on a

2 For more on the sixtyfold test, take a look at three of my books: *The Fire of Delayed Answers*, and, *Pain, Perplexity, and Promotion: A prophetic interpretation of the book of Job*, and, *The Chastening of the Lord.*

team, can't mobilize visionary initiatives, can't visit anytime I want with family or friends at a coffee shop. Sometimes I'm overwhelmed with how far I still must go to reach the higher plane He has for me.

But then at other times, He takes me past a bend on the mountain pass, and I get a glimpse of the winding path below that we've just traversed. In those moments, I seem to get a brief glimpse of the greater fruitfulness He's already begun in my life. For example, over thirty books have come so far from this trial. The Lord has made me fruitful through writing, more than I could have anticipated. And the story's still not over—I'm still waiting for His promised healing of my voice. I'm persuaded the best is yet to come.

Your best is also yet to come. You can be assured that He who started this good work in you will complete it (Phil 1:6).

At the thirtyfold crisis, God was probably teaching you some things you needed to learn. But at the sixtyfold crisis, He's not simply teaching you something, He's training you. He's changing your very DNA. It's not a lesson to be learned, but a journey to be walked.

You'll come through with scars that give authority to every word and deed. If Jesus couldn't overcome Satan without incurring scars, what makes us think we can? But because of His scars, Jesus now holds *all* the keys of the kingdom (see Rev 1:18). There are some keys you must have scars to handle.

Jesus is speaking over your life the same thing the Father spoke over His life at His crucifixion. He's saying to you:

Because he has set his love upon Me, therefore I will deliver him; I will set him on high, because he has known My name. He shall call upon Me, and I will answer him; I will be with him in trouble; I will deliver him and honor him. With long life I will satisfy him, and show him My salvation (Ps 91:14-16).

You're a prisoner of hope (Zech 9:12). What is your hope?

That this fiery trial you're enduring is the sixtyfold test, and when you have passed it and come forth as gold, it will open to new realms of fruitfulness.

Endure in the race! Jesus is leading you into hundredfold fruitfulness!

CHAPTER 26

Summary: Best Practices for Disciples

This final chapter summarizes this book's content. As you review these leading takeaways, you'll be reminded of the essence of the message in the parable of the sower, and will see from a bird's-eye perspective Jesus' model of discipleship. Return to this list repeatedly and pray your way through it. As you follow these practices, you'll become a more fruitful disciple of Christ.

Through the parable of the sower—which is Jesus' template for discipleship—Jesus is calling you to hundredfold fruitfulness.

According to Part One, Jesus is calling you to:

- See all of life through the lens of fruitfulness (Ch 1)
- Desire increasing fruitfulness
- Emulate Jesus in everything
- Bear fruit that *remains*
- Become increasingly fruitful with age
- Always be alert, listening, and watching (Ch 2)
- Love Jesus with wholehearted authenticity (Ch 3)
- Value the eternal over the temporary (Ch 4)
- Seek first that which is eternally fruitful
- Tune your ears to hear every word of Christ (Ch 5)
- Practice seclusion, word immersion, and fasting
- Abide continually in the word of Christ (Ch 6)
- Practice physical exercise but in moderation
- Devote yourself to things that have an eternal reward
- Invest in friendship with Jesus through prayer (Ch 7)
- Develop Christlike character
- Edify and strengthen other believers
- Help other disciples become more fruitful
- Win souls

- Exercise wise financial stewardship
- Carefully obey Jesus (Ch 8)
- Provide security for your household
- Teach your children in the Lord's ways
- Endure persecution
- Glorify God by causing people's esteem of Him to elevate

According to Part Two, Jesus is calling you to:

- Break up hard places of unbelief in your heart (Ch 9)
- Guard against trampling other people (Ch 10)
- Guard against trampling your spouse
- Go after any sin in your marriage
- Rebuke rather than trample your spouse
- Wash in the sprinkled blood and water of the word
- Refuse to be offended, but always forgive (Ch 11)
- Soften your heart after being violated
- Soften your heart after being rejected
- Guard from being trampled by beasts of culture (Ch 12)
- Not allow media platforms to trample you
- Engage the fight of faith against depression
- Receive the unique way Jesus walks with you
- Practice a lifestyle of repentance (Ch 13)
- Weep and mourn for your hard heart
- Practice fasting
- Pray the Scriptures
- Receive the rains of the Holy Spirit

According to Part Three, Jesus is calling you to:

- Dig up any stones of compromise you encounter (Ch 14)
- Refuse to medicate your stones
- Thrust your roots deeply into the love of Christ
- Go after stones of fear, anxiety, and worry (Ch 15)
- Go after stones of anger, hatred, and cynicism (Ch 16)

- Refuse to tolerate addictions
- Go after stones of foolish talking, lying, or racism
- Go after stones of porn and sexual sin
- Bring all your stones into the light

According to Part Four, Jesus is calling you to:

- Continually cut back your weeds (Ch 17)
- Keep cutting back the love of money (Ch 18)
- Distrust your heart when it comes to the allure of money
- Keep cutting back the pleasures of life (Ch 19)
- Keep cutting back desires for stuff
- Always preserve your sense of pilgrimage
- Cut back the weeds of comparison

According to Part Five, Jesus is calling you to:

- Carefully navigate the three stages of maturity (Ch 20)
- Grow past infancy and become young men (Ch 21)
- Pursue the knowledge of God
- Die to self at the Lordship Crisis (Ch 22)
- Endure the losses at the Abandonment Crisis
- Allow the wilderness to purge unbelief (Ch 23)
- Turn loneliness into friendship with Jesus
- Develop spiritual grit in despondency
- Stay in fellowship when relationships get hard
- Say yes to Jesus with every test (Ch 24)
- Pray dangerous prayers, "Whatever it takes"
- Endure unto hundredfold fruitfulness
- Faithfully multiply your talents and abilities (Appendix)
- Combine multiplied talents with hundredfold fruitfulness
- Not despise the talents you've been given
- Pursue world-changing fruitfulness

APPENDIX

Fruitfulness Versus Talents

Someone might say, "I'm only ever going to be a thirtyfold Christian. That's my calling in life." In response, I might say, "Maybe you're confusing fruitfulness with talents."

It's easy to confuse them. In the parable of the talents, Jesus described a master who divided his goods among his servants, giving various servants five talents, two talents, and one talent respectively (Matt 25:14-30). Then the master left them to increase through trading what they were given.

It's easy to suppose that, in the parable of the talents, Jesus was making the same point as the parable of the sower. After all, both parables contain *triads*—in the one parable there's thirty, sixty, and hundredfold; in the other there's five, two, and one talent. Also, both parables share the common value of *increasing* what's been given.

Someone might assume, therefore, that one talent corresponds to thirtyfold, two talents corresponds to sixtyfold, and five talents corresponds to hundredfold fruitfulness. If that were true, one implication would be this: Just as a one-talent person will never become a five-talent person, a thirtyfold person will never become a hundredfold fruitful person.

Not so.

The messages of the two parables are different. True, some people will never become five-talent people, but *every* thirtyfold Christian has a calling to grow in fruitfulness until they become hundredfold fruitful. The calling to hundredfold is universal, regardless of how many talents you've been given.

What are some of the distinctions between the two parables? I'll try to explain, because we'll gain more benefit from both parables when we understand the differences.

In Jesus' day, a talent was typically a valuable and significant weight of silver. In the parable of the talents, various servants received different amounts of silver based on their ability to steward those resources, and then were commissioned to grow their value (Matt 25:14-30).

Applied to our lives, those talents represented gifts and abilities God gives us so we can be productive in life and service for Him. God gives greater strengths and gifts to some than to others. When God gives someone a stronger gift, it's because they have a stronger frame to support and administer that gift. If we were to receive a talent that is heavier than our frame can sustain, that talent would actually wound and break us. God loves us too much to give us talents we can't properly steward.

The main idea in the parable of the talents is stewardship and multiplication. Stewardship always involves accountability. Those who receive more talents have a greater accountability to God for how they steward those talents. When you see someone more talented than you, therefore, you might say to the Lord, "Thank You for not giving me that talent. If You had, it would have hurt me, broken me, and brought me into judgment."

In contrast, the main idea in the parable of the sower is fruitfulness.

The Distinction

What are talents? Talents are varying *capacities* God places in our minds, souls, personalities, and bodies to accomplish meaningful goals. God wants us to work our talents with all our might, grow them, maximize their potential, and produce a compounded return on His generous investment in our lives.

In contrast, what is fruit? Here's a reminder of our working definition: *Spiritual fruit is any godly deposit or quality that makes it into the age to come.* Fruit is grown as a consequence of labors that are consecrated to God. When we labor in obedience to His will, we can produce eternal fruit that pleases God.

Talents refer to abilities and capacities; fruitfulness refers to how effectively we use those talents for eternal value.

To understand the difference between talents and fruitfulness, consider the example of nonbelievers. Nonbelievers are given talents by God, and they can grow two talents into four or five talents into ten. But even though they may be faithful to develop and multiply their talents, they are fruitless before God. It's impossible for nonbelievers to be fruitful to God. Why? Because their hearts are dead to God. They may be very talented, but they're unfruitful.

In other words, it's possible to multiply five talents effectively and yet be fruitless to God. On the other hand, it's possible to have just one talent and yet be exceedingly fruitful before God.

Let me continue to distinguish between talents and fruit.

A one-talent believer can be either thirtyfold, sixtyfold, or hundredfold fruitful. Similarly, a two-talent believer can be either thirtyfold, sixtyfold, or hundredfold fruitful. The same is true for a five-talent believer. We have no choice about the number of talents God gives us, but we do have a choice about becoming more consecrated and fruitful to God.

Fruitfulness is more desirable than talents. You may have just one talent, but don't despise the fruitful potential within that solitary talent. A one-talent disciple functioning in hundredfold fruitfulness is likely to be more effective in the kingdom than a five-talent disciple functioning at thirtyfold fruitfulness. The most significant issue is not how talented you are, but how fruitful you are.

Five talents are not available to all, but hundredfold fruitfulness *is* available to all. The only thing keeping us from hundredfold fruitfulness is our consecration to Christ—that is, our consecration to soften our hearts, remove our stones, and cut back our weeds.

Talents and fruit are measured differently. Our talents are measured in contrast to other people; our fruitfulness, however, is measured against the metrics of our own personal potential. When you measure talents, you might say that Kathy has two talents in comparison to Susan who has five. But when it comes to fruitfulness, you don't compare Kathy and Susan; you compare each individual with their own spiritual potential to bear fruit to God.

We don't evaluate our fruitfulness by looking over at our neighbor's progress; rather, we measure our progress by looking up at the upward call of God on our life.

There's freedom here. When you realize that fruitfulness is more significant than talents, you'll be liberated from the bondage of comparing yourself with others, and you'll enjoy the delight of setting your gaze entirely on the beauty of Christ and His upward call.

Five Talents at Hundredfold Fruitfulness

When five talents combine with hundredfold fruitfulness, the impact for the kingdom can be rather astounding.

I want to illustrate this with five-talent Joseph. I call him a five-talent guy because he was gifted in so many ways—in mind, body, emotions, and personality. He demonstrated the strength of his talents by running Potiphar's entire household and business. Joseph was very fruitful in Potiphar's house, but God wanted more for Joseph—hundredfold fruitfulness. To get him there, God crafted for Joseph a prison.

God put Joseph in prison to excavate his soul and train him for hundredfold fruitfulness. When he finally emerged from prison, Joseph still had his five talents, but now they were combined with hundredfold fruitfulness—and history was changed!

It's rather astonishing to consider how Joseph changed history. He came out of prison at age thirty with wisdom greater than his elders, he became a father to Pharaoh, he made Pharaoh the richest man on the planet, he singlehandedly saved the lives of every individual in the nation of Egypt, and he became a feeder of nations. But that's not all. He left his greatest imprint on human history when he established his family in prosperity in the land of Goshen. From the garden of Goshen, Israel grew into a nation that has shaped and continues to shape world history. Goshen was the crown jewel that demonstrated Joseph's hundredfold fruitfulness.

Yes, Joseph's life illustrates the explosive potential of a five-talent disciple serving at hundredfold fruitfulness. But I also want to show that a one-talent disciple serving at hundredfold fruitfulness can also change human history.

One Talent at Hundredfold Fruitfulness

A one-talent person, even though limited in their talents, has the potential to impact their generation in powerful ways when they attain to hundredfold fruitfulness. To illustrate my meaning, I'm going to the example of Anna, whose impact for the kingdom was truly astounding.

I consider Anna a one-talent woman because she was simple and unsophisticated in her upbringing. There's no indication she was educated in higher learning. Neither was she a skilled businesswoman. I can imagine Anna looking at her one talent and thinking, *Well, at least there's one thing that I can do. I can be a faithful wife and a good mom.*

After seven years of marriage, however, her husband suddenly died. With his death, all hope of raising children also died. Her ability to develop the one talent she possessed seemed to be stripped from her. Bereaved of husband and left childless, she must have thought her legacy would be nothing but barrenness.

But still, even though her one talent was seemingly extinguished, Anna preserved her consecration to God. She served the Lord with fasting and prayer in the temple, night and day.

How did it end? Through her intercessory ministry, she gave birth in a metaphorical way to the Messiah. After decades of intercession, she eventually held in her arms the fruit of her intercession (Luke 2:36-38). A one-talent woman who thought her motherhood was forever stripped from her became, through her devotion to God, a spiritual mother to *millions*. Now *that's* hundredfold fruitfulness!

A one-talent woman ministering to the Lord in hundredfold fruitfulness did more to shape human history than most five-talent people ever do.

Yes, Anna's life illustrates the explosive potential of a one-talent disciple serving at hundredfold fruitfulness. Again, the great value is not the number of talents, but the measure of fruitfulness.

Be encouraged by Anna's example! Whether you're a five-talent, two-talent, or one-talent believer, devote yourself wholeheartedly to hundredfold fruitfulness and you also may change human history.

Fruitful Heart Curriculum

The Fruitful Heart Curriculum consists of two books:

- *SECRETS OF A FRUITFUL HEART*: Tools for Spiritual Growth from Jesus' Parable of the Sower
- Secrets of a Fruitful Heart: *DISCIPLESHIP MANUAL*

SECRETS OF A FRUITFUL HEART is a powerful exploration of Jesus' Parable of the Sower. When used with the *DISCIPLESHIP MANUAL*, these two books are a profound discipleship curriculum.

The wayside soil represents places in our hearts that have been trampled hard. The stones represent pockets of compromise that hinder our roots. The weeds represent cares and pleasures that choke our fruitfulness. With three powerful images, Jesus gave us His model of discipleship. When we soften our hearts, remove our stones, and cut back our weeds, our hearts become increasingly fruitful to God.

The *DISCIPLESHIP MANUAL* is written to help small discipleship groups go deeper in the parable. With each chapter, disciples answer questions that make the parable relevant for our lives. Then, when the group comes together, the Manual provides Discussion Questions that are relevant to every disciple. You'll be surprised at what you learn and discover just by interacting in your group with the questions.

For more information or quantity orders, go to www.FruitfulHeart.net. Make disciples Jesus' way!

Books by Bob Sorge

Discipleship
Secrets of a Fruitful Heart
Secrets of a Fruitful Heart: Discipleship Manual
Secrets of the Secret Place
Secrets of the Secret Place: Companion Study Guide
A Covenant With My Eyes
Stuck: Help for the Troubled Home

Prayer
Secrets of the Secret Place (paperback & hardcover)
Secrets of the Secret Place: Companion Study Guide
Secrets of the Secret Place: Leader's Manual
Reset: 20 Ways to a Consistent Prayer Life
Unrelenting Prayer
Illegal Prayers
Power of the Blood
Minute Meditations

Worship
Exploring Worship: A Practical Guide to Praise and Worship
Exploring Worship Workbook & Discussion Guide
Glory: When Heaven Invades Earth
Following The River: A Vision for Corporate Worship
Next Wave: Worship in a New Era

Enduring Faith
In His Face
The Fire Of Delayed Answers
The Fire Of God's Love
Pain, Perplexity, & Promotion: A Prophetic Interpretation of the Book of Job
Opened From the Inside: Taking the Stronghold of Zion
God's Still Writing Your Story

The Chastening of the Lord: The Forgotten Doctrine
The Cross: Never Too Dead for Resurrection
It's Not a Tomb It's a Womb
Sometimes We Need Trials

Leadership
Dealing With the Rejection and Praise of Man
Envy: The Enemy Within
Loyalty: The Reach Of The Noble Heart
It's Not Business It's Personal

For info on each title, go to oasishouse.com
Call Oasis House at 816-767-8880

Bob's books are also available at:
christianbook.com
amazon.com
Kindle, iBooks, Nook, Google Play
Audible

Stay connected with Bob at:
fruitfulheart.net
oasishouse.com
YouTube.com/bobsorge
Facebook.com/BobSorgeMinistry
Blog: bobsorge.com
Instagram: bob.sorge
Twitter.com/BOBSORGE

Secrets of the Secret Place Curriculum

In addition to the Fruitful Heart Curriculum, Bob Sorge has written another discipleship curriculum that is being used around the world: *SECRETS OF THE SECRET PLACE.*

Bob's Secret Place Curriculum consists of four materials:

1. Secrets of the Secret Place
This book on our quiet time with Jesus is one of the leading resources worldwide for helping believers establish a secret place relationship with Jesus. Available in both paperback and hardcover.

2. Companion Study Guide
The Secrets of the Secret Place Companion Study Guide is useful for both private and group study. Discussion questions help a group engage with the content of each chapter.

3. Secrets Video Course

The secret place video course, taught by Bob Sorge, consists of twelve 30-minute sessions. This video series adds interest to a group study and strengthens the message of the book. The series can be purchased in DVD format, or streamed for free on YouTube—see Bob Sorge's YouTube Channel.

4. Leader's Manual

Almost anyone can lead a group through the Secrets Video Series simply by using the *Leader's Manual.* You'll receive guidelines for leading the group, along with handouts for each person. Photocopy and distribute the handouts for each person to complete while watching the film. The *Leader's Manual* is available in booklet form, or may be downloaded on the *Free Downloads* page at www.oasishouse.com.

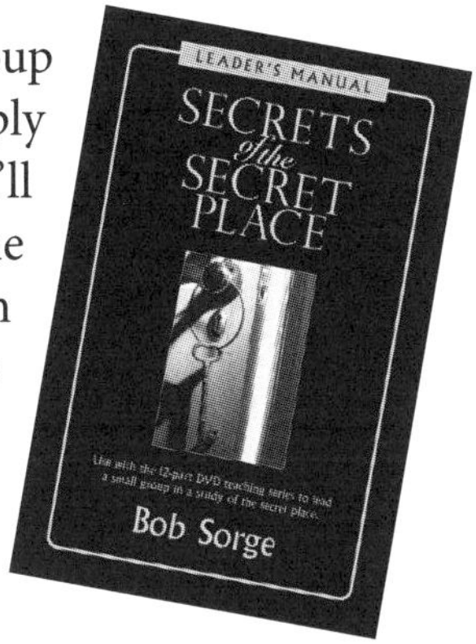

This Secret Place Curriculum is an unparalleled tool for equipping believers in the necessity and magnificence of a secret place relationship with Jesus. Get your small group onto this! www.oasishouse.com